Reel Parables

*Life Lessons
from
Popular Films*

James Hogan

Paulist Press
New York / Mahwah, NJ

Cover design by Sharyn Banks
Book design by Lynn Else

Library of Congress Cataloging-in-Publication Data

Hogan, James, 1959–
    Reel parables : life lessons from popular films / James Hogan.
        p. cm.
    ISBN 978-0-8091-4458-7 (alk. paper)
    1. Motion pictures—Religious aspects—Christianity. 2. Motion pictures—Moral and ethical aspects. I. Title.
    PN1995.5.H595 2008
    261.5′7—dc22

                                                           2007025004

Published by Paulist Press
997 Macarthur Boulevard
Mahwah, New Jersey 07430

www.paulistpress.com

Printed and bound in the
United States of America

Contents

For their gifts of faith and love,
this book is dedicated to
Gene and Nancy Hogan,
my beloved Dad and Mom.

Acknowledgments

Jack may have felled the giant and won the goose that laid the golden eggs, but he couldn't have done anything without the beanstalk. Any giant insights or golden truths that I may have stumbled upon in the writing of *Reel Parables* could never have been found without the support of my friends and family. Like the beanstalk, they have lifted me up. And so, as in the partaking of a dinner, the thanks should always come first.

I wish to thank my Mom and Dad for their love, which has been as constant as the seasons. I can dedicate this book to them because they first dedicated their lives to me. No better imitator of Mary and Joseph could I have had.

My thanks to my beautiful and wonderful wife, Colleen, for her faith, her intellect, and her love; to my children, Clare, Kate, Erin, Thomas, and Meg, who are my greatest blessings on God's green earth; to my big brothers John and Mike, to my sisters Kathleen and Maureen, and all my nieces and nephews, especially David and Ted, whom I was honored to teach.

My thanks to the Irish O'Malley clan as well; to the amazing John and Kay, and to the greatest compilation of baby-sitters in the western hemisphere, including Maureen, Peggy, Mary Jo, Shawn, Kathleen, and Dennis. Especially, my thanks to Ed Winters, who has been so supportive of my writing for all the right reasons.

To the theological gang at Ignatius—Jim Skerl, Tom Healey, Jim Brennan, Dan Galla, Karl Ertle, Father Larry Ober, SJ, Marty Dybicz, Joe Ptak, Gayle Scaravilli, Father Ray Guiao, SJ, Mike McLaughlin, Brendan Sammon, and Drew Vilinsky—my eternal appreciation for the privilege of working with you. My special thanks to our "angelic doctor," Michael Pennock, who taught us so that we might teach others in the imitation of Christ; and especially to my friend Paul Prokop, who spent many an hour reading and critiquing this book to make it 100 percent better. To brilliant colleagues like you, I can only "pay it forward."

The family of God extends far and wide. My gratitude also goes to Pat Corrigan, Luigi Pecarara, Francis Brewka, Thad Coreno, and Paul Fisher, the best of friends—and most especially to Tom Becks for his companionship and inspiration.

I am grateful for fathers in faith such as Father Tim Kesicki, SJ, Father Tom Webber, and to Sister Jeanne Tighe, SFCC, and Sister Dianne Selva, SFCC, for their incredible support of my family and me.

Most especially, my gratitude goes to Father Lawrence Boadt, CSP, and his team of editors, particularly Paul McMahon, for bringing these words to the people, in the hopes of spreading the good news.

I write these words of praise with the firm conviction that in every person I thank, it is God who is ultimately praised.

Prologue

James Hogan Productions (2007)

"C'mon Mr. Hogan, do you have to find theology in everything? It's just a movie. It's just a movie. It's just a movie...." I can hear the ghosts of students past echoing these words, even as I write them. I can't completely blame my students. I have been known to use Pez to explain the divinity of Christ and M&Ms to defend racial equality. I have used the invasion of Normandy to promote Christmas and piggy banks to illustrate the Catholic Church. My track record on "strange" is fairly well established. Fortunately, what appears to be a strange connection can still be a true connection, as it is between theology and movies. Theology is the study of God, the Architect of everything. Therefore, everything falls under the auspices of theology, even Pez, piggy banks, and, especially for this book, movies.

Reel Parables is a book about Christian truths that are illustrated in popular films. I intentionally avoided movies about overtly religious topics, such as *Jesus of Nazareth* or *The Robe,* because I believe that movies in which the Christian message is somewhat hidden can be more powerful, reaching out to a wider group of viewers who may be predisposed to miss or reject traditional religious faith.

We probably all know people who will not set foot in a church but who regularly go to the movies. For some the theater is an escape from religion, a place where they effectively replace bread and wine with popcorn and a soda. But God is bigger than the confines of any church building. God's ways are mysterious. God seeks his own cracks of entry into our lived experience, even when we consciously shut him out. God can weave his way onto the silver screen.

For others, religious insight is exactly what they are seeking by entering a theater. In addition to entertainment, they hope for a fresh perspective that will last long after the film is finished. They are not just looking for a good time; they are looking for a way to make their lifetime good.

Abstract artists like Picasso are hailed for being able to show in their art a unique way of looking at reality. This certainly has some value, though it is not new. Everyone already has a unique point of view. Picasso was able to objectify his perspective into art. Consequently, what he mostly taught us about was Picasso—his own radical perspective was the value that the onlookers prized. Modern art, like modern philosophy, begins with the self. And the worst of modern art ends with the self as well. That is why much of modern art is not art at all. But for artists like Michelangelo and Leonardo da Vinci, it was the truth that the art mediated to the patron that they valued, not themselves. They saw that their task was to use their talent to get out of the way of the art. In other words, Michelangelo hoped that when we gaze at his *Pietà,* we would ponder Mary holding the crucified Jesus, not Michelangelo.

Michelangelo understood what many contemporary artists do not: art is essentially religious. Art is not "divine madness," as Plato described it. More accurately, art is "divine sanity," helping us break out of the prison of our own thoughts, our own selfishness. We are tapping into the power of the Creator when we subcreate a work of art or behold a work of art. Applying this to film, the best of them have power—a power that, if used well, can give us insights that are greater than the film, stories that point to a greater truth. Art should point beyond itself, because we are meant to point beyond ourselves toward our Creator.

In his essay "On Fairy-Stories," J. R. R. Tolkien wrote about the nature and purpose of story. When we create a story, Tolkien said, we take elements of the real world, such as the green of trees and the white of snow, and then, using our imagination, we combine them together to create a secondary world that our mind can enter. And if the storyteller is particularly skilled in his craft, we become temporarily "lost" in the imaginative world of his creation. When the magician's spell is complete, we reconnect with the primary world once again. But the enchantment has had its effect. The story, if it is truthful, can help us rediscover forgotten truths and see those truths in a new light.

It makes sense that the God who shaped the story of the world would give the power of story to us. Our creativity flows from God; therefore it can fit into divine purposes. Jesus, God incarnate, did the same thing during his public ministry. A master storyteller, Jesus took ordinary images to which the people of his time could relate—a farmer in his field, a father and son relationship, or a man who falls among thieves—and used them to unlock the mystery of the kingdom of God, bringing a better understanding of heaven to earth, ordinary stories that shed light on the extraordinary God. Jesus used the secular images of his day to conjure up in the mind of his listeners a fresh understanding of God as our loving Father—good news that would inevitably point toward the ultimate Storyteller. Each parable helped unlock a door to a new and exciting secret garden.

Similarly, the settings of the films featured in this book—a baseball field, outer space, a basketball court, a college, a small town, or even a made-up world like Middle-earth—are as secular as Jesus' parables, but God, hidden beneath the surface, reveals himself in the telling. They are "reel parables" from the silver screen.

Film as parable? To be sure, the notion that God and story are intimately related would be laughed at by most Hollywood moguls, actors, and critics. Much of Hollywood ignores questions of theology or morality in art, allowing a good deal of contemporary art to become the propaganda machine of secularism. We cannot let them off the hook too easily. They can run from God but they can't hide. Theology is simply thought applied to faith, and faith is unavoidable. Even atheism, the belief that God does not exist, is still a belief—an intellectual leap of faith that the atheist makes to believe in the validity of his or her own thoughts. Every screenwriter and moviemaker has a theological point of view, a life philosophy that inevitably is incorporated into the text and context of the story, whether they are aware of it or not, and that point of view is projected (pardon the pun) to the viewer. As the audience, we absorb the theology that is in a story whether or not we are conscious of it.

This book is not a collection of lesson plans for teachers who want to show films, or a Roger Ebertlike book of critical reviews. This book takes on topics where critics fear to tread, into the moral and religious areas of life that really matter to ordinary people. Regular people talk about movies quite differently from the way movie critics do. A movie critic is a person who judges the quality of a restaurant pizza after he has just finished consuming ten. That pizza can never satisfy him in the way it might satisfy an average person who hasn't had a pizza in a month. Too many movie critics are interested in what is new, not in what is eternal. Their comments are more about the artistic style of the film than the substance. And when the substance of the story is discussed, it is usually devoid of any moral or religious depth. These omissions are made either out of cowardice (they are afraid to be unpopular) or ignorance (they believe that morals and religion can be separated from public life and art.)

Fortunately, the common person is more interested in truth than in novelty. It is for such persons that this book has been written. This book is for everyone, written by an everyman. It is the conversation *after* the movie. (Caution: This book is, therefore, a spoiler.) It is a companion to the film, to enhance the viewing experience.

Think of this book as baptizing what is considered secular by revealing what is sacred in a story. Why wouldn't we want art to be Christianized, to be made holy? That's what we do. Christianity declares sacred what Christ has already made holy. Christ had already given us the winter solstice; we gave it back to him as Christmas. Christ had already made the ancient isle of Ireland; we gave it back to him as Catholic.

Christian art doesn't have to speak about Jesus in order to be Christian. It has to possess the truth that is Jesus in order to be

Christian. Just as with a real Christian, Christ dwells in his heart, soul, and strength, so, too, Christian art is any art that makes Christ known. He can live in the body of the work, behind the words and through the images, just as he dwells within our bodies and souls. Great films are not about Oscar or Emmy, but about Jesus—whether they overtly mention him or not. The greatest story ever told is the greatest story retold—over and over again. Through the power of story art, the good news can resonate with viewers who don't recognize the cross of Christ as the zenith of self-sacrifice in human history.

And just as we are not perfect temples for Christ to dwell in, the twenty movies discussed in this book are far from perfect as well. Many, like *The Shawshank Redemption* and *The Lord of the Rings,* contain excessive violence and/or vulgar language. *Rain Man* contains unnecessary vulgar language. *Amadeus* (in the director's cut) contains very brief scenes of nudity. *Forrest Gump* and *Groundhog Day* contain sexual situations. Despite their flaws, the stories nonetheless convey powerful truths.

In *Amadeus,* the royal court forbids the composer Mozart to perform the opera *The Marriage of Figaro.* Mozart declares out of frustration, "Why must we go on forever writing only about gods and legends?" The emperor's counselor replies, "Because they do; they go on forever. At least, what they represent—the eternal in us. Opera is here to enable us, Mozart. Not just the emperor, but all the people." Applying the counselor's wisdom to *Reel Parables,* one might ask, "Why must we go on forever reading about God and humanity?" Because they do, they go on forever. God and the people of God, and, to a certain extent, the stories themselves, can go on forever. Timeless truths are always needed just in time. They jolt us out of our own life experience to consider another's. Through the power of story, we not only can walk a mile in another man's shoes, but we can try on his hat and coat as well. When we vicariously enter into a character, as she learns, we learn. When the movie ends and the theater lights come back on, we can be the ones enlightened as we walk out of the theater.

At the risk of alienating the strict composition teachers in the country, the *I* point of view is occasionally inserted throughout this book, for good reason. Unlike writing on mathematics or language, religion involves the totality of the human person. Anyone who has ever taught theology to a student, child, or friend knows that the personal witness value is more important than the content. Theology cannot be taught or written without witnessing personal faith, and I didn't want to convey the illusion of cold objectivity where none exists. The false impression of completely detached objectivity was lost with the mindset of Newtonian physics. Let it remain so. I cannot divorce my head from my heart, my reason from my faith.

In each chapter, I will try to frame the story in the light of Christian faith. There is much wealth to be had in them. Each is as different as a sapphire is to an emerald, but all reflect a common beauty. They make us want to be better than we are. They offer not only entertainment, but also happiness. Entertained is how we feel when we are watching them. Happiness is what we experience when the film is over. With so many modern films filled with empty calories, these twenty are spiritually vitamin-enriched. They can lift us up, to personalize a truth, to reveal our goodness—in other words, to inspire.

These stories remind us that we are human, made in the image and likeness of God. They remind us that there is beauty in the world and in ourselves. They reopen old doors to gardens long since closed and partially forgotten, as well as to gardens of which we've never dreamed. They help us see things as they are in a fresh light, as we once saw them when we were children. Experiencing a great movie is like being awakened, refreshed and renewed, after a good night's sleep. A story is a door to a secret garden through which we might enter the kingdom of God. May we enter together.

1

Star Wars Episode IV: A New Hope

BE A FORCE FOR GOODNESS.

LucasFilm Ltd. / 20th Century-Fox (1977)

Producer	Gary Kurtz / George Lucas
Director	George Lucas
Author of Screenplay	George Lucas
Running Time	121 minutes

MAIN CHARACTERS

Luke Skywalker	Mark Hamill
Han Solo	Harrison Ford
Princess Leia Organa	Carrie Fisher
Obi-Wan "Ben" Kenobe	Alec Guinness
Darth Vader	David Prowse/James Earl Jones

George Lucas never forgot his childhood memory of watching the Flash Gordon movie serial on *Adventure Theater*. After directing the critical and box-office success, *American Graffiti,* he outlined his own space opera, complete with starships, lightsabers, heroic knights, a fair princess in distress, strange aliens, and a cosmic battle between good and evil. He entitled the first act *Star Wars.* The rest is movie history.

From a production standpoint, *Star Wars* did not appear to be destined for popular success. Many major studios rejected Lucas's proposal before 20th Century-Fox accepted. *Star Wars* was made with a low budget of $10 million. With the exception of Alec Guinness, Lucas signed virtually no major Hollywood actors. (Harrison Ford was unknown at the time.) He hired young, untested special effects designers. Lucas produced, directed, and wrote the entire film. Far from being a guaranteed moneymaker, for George Lucas, *Star Wars* was more a personal fulfillment, a labor of love.

Star Wars premiered in 1977 to American audiences tired of double-digit inflation, recession, and gas shortages. The audience's response was nothing short of astounding. Although highbrow critics dismissed it, the people loved it. They not only enjoyed the film, they also identified with it. They bought clothing, costumes, toys, action figures, posters, novelizations, illustrated comic books—anything connected to *Star Wars*. It became a phenomenon, one of the first of what is now called the *blockbuster* hit. For the next twenty-five years, subsequent films and product marketing have kept *Star Wars* a part of the American pop-culture landscape.

Star Wars was an escapist fantasy with groundbreaking science-fiction special effects that marked a whole new direction in moviemaking. The characters were both interesting and engaging, and the setting was literally out of this world. But most importantly, it had a classic, quixotic plot line. And it is the story that propels *Star Wars* into the category of American mythology.

The film begins with the now-familiar line, "A long time ago in a galaxy far, far away...." It is the story of Luke Skywalker, a boy on the verge of manhood, not just searching for a career path in life, but for an identity. He is looking for something in which to believe. He comes to find it, not in some present-day trend or future innovation, but in the traditions of the past, as presented by the wise Obi-Wan "Ben" Kenobi. Ben Kenobi was a Jedi knight, just as Luke's father had been before he was killed. Now, the old republic is gone, with the federation of planets controlled by an emperor. Ben reveals to Luke that a former Jedi, Darth Vader, turned to evil and murdered his father.

But Obi-Wan Kenobi is not interested in giving Luke merely a history lesson. He needs Luke's help to deliver stolen plans to rebel forces working against the empire. Even more than that, Obi-Wan wants Luke to follow in the path of the Jedi.

> I have something here for you. Your father wanted you to have this when you were old enough, but your uncle wouldn't allow it. He feared you might follow old Obi-Wan on some damn-fool idealistic crusade like your father did. It's your father's lightsaber. This is the weapon of a Jedi knight. Not as clumsy or as random as a blaster, but an elegant weapon for a more civilized age. For over a thousand generations, the Jedi knights were the guardians of peace and justice in the old republic. Before the dark times, before the empire.

Obi-Wan teaches Luke that the struggle between the rebellion and the empire is only a manifestation of a spiritual struggle between good and evil, articulated in Jedi theology as the light and dark sides of the Force. As Obi-Wan explains, "The Force is what gives a Jedi his power. It's an energy field created by all living things. It surrounds us and penetrates us. It binds the galaxy together."

If the Force is a created thing, then there is someone far greater than the Force, the Creator of all living things, out of which the Force arises. Theologically speaking, Luke would have been better off relating to him. The Force is akin to the ancient Greek gods, who sprang up out of the chaos that existed before them. The Greek gods are created and are therefore not God at all. Neither is the Force. The Force is also impersonal, whereas the God revealed by Christianity is personal. What Lucas may have seen as an advanced philosophy actually amounts to a vague, pantheistic, feelings-oriented theology. But theologic aside, for *Star Wars,* faith in the Force is analogous to faith in God. However weak the thinking might be, by inserting the Force into the storyline, George Lucas brought a religious dimension to *Star Wars.* It is one of the key elements behind the story's appeal. The Force equates to a spiritual reality that interfaces with life, one that Luke accepts—and Han Solo doubts.

Most children, being naturally more idealistic and noble, can initially identify with Luke Skywalker. Adults, more mindful of how principles can be compromised, can more easily relate to Han Solo.

Han Solo is the realistic Huck Finn to Luke's romantic Tom Sawyer character. Portrayed with humor and wit by Harrison Ford, he is perhaps the most lovable character in *Star Wars*. A smuggler of illegal trade, he is on the run from bounty hunters. Although he has no great love for the empire, he is not wholeheartedly on the side of the rebels either. Han is looking out for "number one." Han is a "solo" act. He is tough and worldly, a rascal with a heart of gold, but he would prefer the gold in his pocket. He only gives Luke and Obi-Wan passage on board his ship, the *Millennium Falcon,* as part of a business transaction. He then agrees to assist them in rescuing Princess Leia, who is being held prisoner on the imperial ship, in exchange for reward money. Han is involved, but he is not committed to the cause. But when decent persons don't commit to act against injustice, even in nonviolent ways, evil flourishes and gains power, as is depicted by the empire's construction of the *death star,* a weapon they will use to enslave millions, perhaps even Han.

Han Solo's ambivalent attitude toward religion is indicative of many in our world today. When Luke is being instructed by Obi-Wan in the ways of the Force, Han remarks:

> "Hokey religions and ancient weapons are no match for a good blaster at your side."
>
> "You don't believe in the Force, do you?"
>
> "Kid, I've flown from one side of this galaxy to the other. I've seen a lot of strange stuff, but I've never seen anything that would make me believe there is one all-powerful force controlling everything. There's no mystical energy field that controls my destiny. It's just simple tricks and nonsense."

Han intellectually rejects the reality of God, yet he acts according to principle enough to indicate that his heart is open to the presence of God—more than he would like to admit. Unlike Luke, Obi-Wan and Princess Leia, who represent the clear choice for good, and Darth Vader and the emperor, who represent the clear choice for evil, Han is caught somewhere in the middle. His ambivalence is symbolically represented in the colors he wears. Luke and Leia dress in white, Vader in black, but Han wears both white and black.

Halfhearted faith translates into halfhearted ideals. Without rooted spiritual and moral convictions, it is much more difficult for Han Solo to bring himself to commit fully to the fight against the empire. Like so many of us, Han would rather immerse himself in day-to-day details. Life is complicated enough for him without adding a spiritual and moral dimension to it. His ambivalence toward religion translates into a moral ambivalence as well. The truth is, of course, that none of us can add a spiritual and moral dimension to our lives. It is already there; it exists objectively. We can only subtract it from our lives, and that subtraction is what makes life so complicated, at best, and miserable, at worst.

Han Solo has the mind of a cynic, but the heart of a believer. Part of him wants to live for himself, but another part wants to believe in something greater than himself. His attraction to Princess Leia reveals to himself his true nature, for he admires her spirit, her courage in fighting for justice. She challenges his better self. She makes him want to be a better man.

Much of the film's appeal comes from its being a simple adventure story. It has a setting so fantastic that it can't be easily identified with any political war raging in the real world, and it has a theology so nebulous that it cannot be identified with any partic-ular organized religion. The post-Vietnam generation of the late 1970s, watching *Star Wars* for the first time, could deal with the abstract question of good versus evil without being confused by politics. Freed from political and denominational confusion, they could freshly renew their belief in upholding the fundamental prin-ciples of faith and moral action. This remains true for every new generation of viewers. *Star Wars* pulls each increasingly secularized generation back to the sacred. It reaffirms on an unconscious level the nobility of what traditional faith has always proclaimed: there is a spiritual reality that can help us discover who we are. *Star Wars* answers the essential question of the existence of a spiritual and moral realm with a resounding *yes!* Herein lies its appeal.

Obi-Wan teaches Luke to discern the presence of the Force because he knows that it is ultimately the only hope for victory over the empire. Luke is taught to "trust his feelings" in order to find the Force. However, since feelings are often determined by circumstances outside our control, and are both temporary and misguiding, we would do well to "trust our reasoning" to guide our feelings in religious matters, particularly in discerning the nature of evil.

In *Star Wars,* good and evil are clearly defined. But in life, discerning between them is not so clear. Just as Darth Vader wears a mask that hides his real appearance, so, too, evil masks itself as good in order to deceive us. We choose evil because we don't fully know it as evil; we think it will do us some good.

Nor is evil an equal power to good. The opposite of God is not Satan. The opposite of God is nothing. The opposite of Satan, the fallen angel, is Michael, the archangel. God could destroy evil without drawing a breath or raising a finger. But he won't. God enjoys his own acts of goodness. Having shared life with his creation, God willed humanity to experience creative goodness so that in a small way it would know the joy God knows when God creates.

Possessing the power to choose goodness, we also have the capacity to abuse what is good and cause evil. That is why the battle between good and evil exists. God allows evil, temporarily, because he made us free. Freedom provides the opportunity for love and with love comes our greatest joy. Our refusal to love has been humanity's greatest tragedy. Why doesn't God do something about the problem of evil? He has. God made us. The fundamental choice between good and evil is not the exclusive subject of fantasy. It is the subject of meaningful story only because it is a reality for us. This is one war that does not dwell only in the stars—in a galaxy far, far away. It rages in the here and now—in our brothers, in our sisters, and in ourselves. It is as near as family and neighbor, as close as our own heart.

Obi-Wan represents an ancient vision of reality, one that has been kept from Luke as much as it has been kept from many people today in this ever more secularized world. Darth Vader, to a certain extent, acknowledges that reality. He is no secularist, who limits himself to the material world. When his military officers delight in the construction of the death star, Vader warns, "Don't be too proud of this technological terror you've constructed. The ability to destroy a planet is insignificant next to the power of the Force." His words are ironic considering he has become more a technological machine than man. Although he can acknowledge the spiritual dimension, the absence of love in Darth Vader has distorted the truth regarding the nature of evil. The dark side is the wrong side.

In contrast, Obi-Wan Kenobi has a lived awareness of the creative spiritual reality. He is a Jedi knight in service to the Force. He wishes to have this strength, this presence, reborn in Luke. But Obi-Wan does not teach with words alone; he lives out his belief in the ultimate power of goodness. In his lightsaber battle with Darth Vader, he says, "You can't win, Darth. If you strike me down, I shall become more powerful than you could possibly imagine." Although Vader strikes Obi-Wan down, Luke, spiritually speaking, takes him to heart. Alive in spirit and memory, he is even more an influence on young Luke. It is Obi-Wan who guides Luke, along with Han Solo and Princess Leia, in their escape from the imperial ship.

Having escaped Darth Vader, they deliver the stolen plans to the rebel forces. The plans identify a weakness in the death star that makes it vulnerable to a single, strategically placed photon torpedo. They must attack and destroy the death star before it destroys the rebellion. Luke volunteers to join in the attack. Han, having received his reward, is ready to go his own way. Before engaging the mission to destroy the death star, Luke challenges Han:

> "Come on! Why don't you take a look around? You know what's about to happen, what they're up against. They

could use a good pilot like you. You're turning your back on them."

"What good's a reward if you ain't around to use it? Besides, attacking that battle station ain't my idea of courage. It's more like suicide."

"All right. Well take care of yourself, Han. I guess that's what you're best at, isn't it?"

"Hey Luke—may the Force be with you."

The adventure had made a difference to Han. His last words to Luke reveal the beginnings of belief. But will his belief translate into commitment? In the end, Han Solo makes the right choice, beyond his own self-interest. Before Luke is able to fire a deathblow to the death star, his starfighter is targeted by Darth Vader's ship. But at the last second, the *Millennium Falcon* knocks Vader's ship off course. Han arrives in time. His involvement has become personal, not merely for personal profit. His decision is pivotal in the story, for it makes Luke's victory against the death star possible.

Guided by the spirit of Obi-Wan Kenobi, Luke trusts in the Force, takes aim, and destroys the death star. Obi-Wan tells him, "The Force will be with you, always." The rebels win the battle. Hope is restored to the galaxy.

The subtitle to *Star Wars* is "Episode IV: A New Hope." Luke Skywalker is the new hope, as is every youth today. He does not escape his destiny; he embraces it. He lives out a relationship with the Force greater than himself, upholding the values of love and justice. Han Solo chooses the same. Although their faith is far from the faith of Christianity, there are some parallels in *Star Wars* for the Christian today. What are Christians, after all, but knights in service to the King of Kings? What are Christians, after all, but men and women who experience the force and presence of God? What are Christians but men and women who take ancient, timeless truths and make them alive once again in their hearts? Christianity is a rebellion of love against an enemy that has usurped this world and made it into, as C. S. Lewis wrote, "enemy-occupied territory."

Just as Obi-Wan challenges Luke to accept a reality that was lived out in the past, *Star Wars* challenges us to reassert in our present lives the spiritual reality of God and live with justice. Even the Han Solos of the world must choose sides: the kingdom of God or the primacy of self, the cause of good or the deception of evil, selfless love or sinful misery, the pursuit of justice or the conquest of power. There is no middle ground. Jedi knights, arise!

2

Superman

JESUS IS THE DREAM COME TRUE.

Alexander Salkind / Warner Brothers (1978)

Producer	Alexander Salkind
Director	Richard Donner
Authors of Screenplay	Mario Puzo/David Newman
Running Time	143 minutes

MAIN CHARACTERS

Superman	Christopher Reeve
Lois Lane	Margot Kidder
Jor-El	Marlon Brando
Lex Luthor	Gene Hackman

In 1933, two teenage boys from Cleveland, Ohio, Jerry Siegel and Joe Shuster, came up with a unique idea for a comic book—the first superhero. He would be clothed in tights to make him seem futuristic (which at the time was the style in science-fiction illustrations), given a cape in order to give the effect of motion, and inked in bright red and blue colors. They spent the next few years refining their concept and trying to get it published. Finally, in the summer of 1939, the same year as the invasion of Poland and the start of the Second World War, *Superman #1* debuted—Superman was born.

The combination of unique powers and abilities, a secret identity, and the noble fight for truth and justice, made the Superman saga an immediate favorite. Over time, Superman has become one of the most recognizable images in America, appearing in Sunday comics, magazines, animation, radio, movie serials, television, and finally in 1978, a feature film.

What Hercules was for the Greek imagination, or Beowulf to the medieval mind, Superman is for many Americans today. Although born on the humble illustrated pages of a comic book, Superman is quintessential American mythology.

When an artist subcreates a secondary world, he uses his imagination, which has been influenced by religion and culture. Jerry Siegel, a Jewish-American boy growing up in the 1930s, invented his ideal superman by borrowing from what had already shaped his imagination.

Superman is the Greek ideal of external beauty and physical strength—a body like that of Apollo. In addition to gods and men, Greek mythology also included heroes. They were the offspring of gods and human mothers, like Hercules, Theseus, or Perseus, who would use their abilities to fight monsters and save damsels in distress. Similarly, Superman does not represent mere power; he stands for using power to serve ideals that mirror the American ideal of truth and justice for all. Thus, Superman is the blending of the ideals of classic mythology and American culture, as Siegel understood them.

But myths do not only shape the culture; they also play an important role in forming a person's religious imagination, a role more important than some might ever suspect.

"Myths are lies, though breathed in silver," C. S. Lewis once proclaimed at The Eagle and Child pub in Oxford, when the subject of mythology came up. But he was corrected by a fellow Oxford professor by the name of J. R. R. Tolkien, who pointed out that this was an imaginative failure on Lewis's part. He went on to explain to Lewis that all myths and stories are man functioning as a subcreator. They illustrate the good dreams and desires of humanity, which have been implanted in us by the Creator. The consolation that they offer us, of having our good dreams come true in the imaginary world, will be made true by God in the real world. In fact, in the good news of Jesus Christ, the mythological hope for a hero that would defeat sin, evil, and death *has* come true. The ideal has become real. Referring to the gospel, Tolkien wrote: "There is no tale ever told that men would rather find was true, and none which so many skeptical men have accepted true on its own merits."

Tolkien's insights changed Lewis's mind, and his life—for shortly after that discussion, Lewis became a Christian. Lewis described his conversion experience as "like when a man, after long sleep, still lying motionless in bed, becomes aware that he is now awake." In explaining why he decided to accept the gospel story as truth, Lewis wrote:

> There was no such historical claim (in Hindu mythology) as in Christianity. I was by now too experienced in literary criticism to regard the Gospels as myths. They had not the mythical taste. And yet the very matter which they set down in their artless, historical fashion—those narrow, unattractive Jews, too blind to the mythical wealth of the pagan world around them—was precisely the matter of the great myths. If ever a myth had become fact, had been incarnated, it would be just like this.[1]

> Now the story of Christ is simply a true myth: a myth working on us in the same way as the others, but with this tremendous difference that it really happened: and one must be content to accept in the same way, remembering that it is God's myth where the others are men's myths: i.e. the Pagan stories are God expressing Himself through the minds of poets, using such images as He found there, while Christianity is God expressing Himself through what we call "real things."[2]

The gospel is myth become fact—a moment in actual history, yet also the perfect mythological story. It is a dream that has really come true. The story of Jesus is the pinnacle where two God-shaped slopes reach together—mythology and history. All previous history and mythology served to prepare the way for the story of

Jesus. All subsequent mythology, including Superman, harkens back to *the* spiritual pinnacle of human history.

This is why story matters so much, no matter whether it is as profound as a Greek tragedy, a Shakespeare play, an epic poem, or as mundane as a television sit-com, a cheap novel, or a superhero comic book. All of these stories shape our imaginations, either closer to the good news of Jesus Christ or further away from it. To the extent that these stories mirror the story of Christ, they move us closer to *the* Superman who has come to save us and set us free.

To a certain extent, all heroic stories reflect the heroic life of Jesus—the hero's sense of mission, taking the risk to love, fighting for justice, facing death and surviving, and so on. But whether consciously written or not, the parallels between the story of Superman and Jesus are even stronger. The greatest story ever told continues to be the greatest story ever retold:

Prior to his journey to earth, there is a revolt led by General Zod and his minions to gain absolute control of Krypton. The three criminals of Krypton who tried to overthrow the ordered world are sentenced to an "eternal living death" in the Phantom Zone.

Prior to human history, there was a revolt led by Satan and his minions to gain absolute control of heaven. The demons that tried to overthrow God's kingdom were sentenced to an "eternal living death" in hell. Hell is the Phantom Zone—where we are but a mere phantom of what we once were.

The story of Superman begins with a Kryptonian family of three (trinity)—Jor-el, Lar-el, and Kal-el (*El* is the Hebrew word for God.) Superman's nonearthly father sends his only son to earth, saying, "The son becomes the father, the father... the son."

The story of Jesus began in the Trinitarian God—Father, Son, and Spirit. God the Father sends His only Son to earth. The Son is begotten, not made, one in being with the Father. "Do you not believe that I am in the Father and the Father is in me?" (John 14:10)

Superman remains magically connected to his "heavenly"

Jesus remains mystically connected to his heavenly Father.

father. "He will not be alone, he will never be alone."

"The Father and I are one." (John 10:30)

Kal-el becomes Clark Kent, the adopted child of Martha and Jonathan Kent, who raise him in Smallville, the moral heartland of America. Clark's father dies when he is young, before his public ministry begins. As he grows up, Superman comes to realize his special mission to save the people of Earth.

The Son of God became Jesus, the child of Mary and his adopted father Joseph, who raised him in the small town of Nazareth, in Judaic faith and morals. We assume that Joseph died before Jesus' public ministry had begun. As he grew steadily in wisdom and knowledge before God, Jesus accepted his personal mission to save the people of Earth from the slavery of sin.

Upon reaching adulthood, Clark's father reveals himself through the power of green crystal, teaching him, "They can be a great people, Kal-el, if they wish to be. They only lack the light to show them the way. For this reason, above all, their capacity for good, I have sent them you, my only son."

Upon reaching adulthood, Jesus' heavenly Father publicly revealed himself in Jesus' baptism, proclaiming, "This is my Son, the Beloved, with whom I am well pleased." (Matt 3:17)

Superman goes into the arctic wilderness in solitude to fathom his true identity and purpose, before beginning his public ministry. "You are here for a reason," his father had told him. Superman learns that his powers are for service, not for personal gain.

Jesus went into the desert wilderness in solitude to confirm his true identity and purpose, before beginning his public ministry. While in the desert, Satan tempted Jesus by saying: "All these I will give you, if you will fall down and worship me." (Matt 4:9) Jesus understood that his powers were for service, not for personal gain.

Superman maintains his secret identity as Clark Kent, mild-mannered newspaper reporter—an identity that is known to us, the reader.

Jesus, at first, kept his identity secret to many, but slowly revealed it as the disciples' faith grew. It is now known to us, the believer.

Beginning his public ministry, particularly in the big city of Metropolis, Superman, the last son of Krypton, performs wonders that astonish the people. When Air Force One is hit by lightning, Superman calms the airline crew and guides the airplane through the storm. When Lois Lane asks him, "Who are you?" Superman answers, "A friend."

Superman invites Lois Lane to learn more about him, so that she might tell the world about his mission. He invites Lois to share in his superhuman abilities and join him in flight. (At one point, she falls downward, only to be caught up again by Superman.)

Superman's archenemy is *Lex Luthor*, who dwells in an underground hideout. Luthor boldly proclaims his worldly achievements to Superman.

Lex Luthor is not an equal to Superman. He possesses none of Superman's otherworldly abilities. He holds only earthly power—money, intellect, and fame. Although Superman has the power to place himself in command of the world, he chooses to serve as his father had served before him. Luthor despises Superman because he

Beginning his public ministry, particularly in the big city of Jerusalem, Jesus, the only Son of God, performed wonders that astonished the people. When the disciples were caught on a boat in a storm, Jesus calmed the waters and guided the disciples through the storm. Jesus said to his disciples, "I have called you friends." (John 15:15)

Jesus invited Peter, James, and John to learn more about him, so they might tell the world about his mission. He invited Peter to share in his miraculous abilities and join him in walking on water. (At one point, he slipped downward, only to be pulled back up by Jesus).

Jesus' enemy was the archdemon *Lucifer*, who dwelled in the underworld. The name *Lucifer* means *bearer of light,* an ironic name for the Prince of Darkness. Lucifer boldly proclaimed his worldly power to Jesus in the desert.

Lucifer was not an equal to Jesus. He possessed none of Jesus' divine attributes. A fallen angel, he held only the allure of earthly power—money, intellect, and fame. Although Jesus had the power to place himself in command of the world, he chose to serve as his heavenly Father serves. Christ's life was a new testament to God and the has the power to achieve what Luthor has always aspired to achieve, yet refuses. It is Superman's capacity for goodness that resonates with the viewer and creates the expectation of a happy ending. We long to see good triumph over evil.

inevitable triumph of his goodness. Good and evil have never been equal forces in the universe. Christ's death and resurrection were the beginning of humanity's "happy ending and the inevitability of the triumph of good over evil."

At the story's triumphant ending, Superman flies into the heavens, watching over his beloved planet. And it is only the beginning.

At the gospel's triumphant ending, Jesus ascended into heaven, promising that he would be with them always. And it was only the beginning.

When *Superman* premiered in 1978, it was the first major motion picture about a superhero, and it paved the way for many others, including *Batman, Spiderman,* and *X-Men.* Produced before the computer age of digital special effects, it was, nonetheless, the visual delight of its day. I was a freshman in college when I first saw it at a movie theater, and I loved it. My friend and I went to see it eight times! (This was before the home videocassette recorder.) There was something about the story that appealed to me—its childlike idealism, its wholesomeness, its goodness. And there was one other thing—Superman could fly.

We identify with a character like Superman because he evokes in us a longing to someday be like him. We wish to *fly*—to defy the confines of gravity—not with a plane or rocket, but simply by pure will. We wish to no longer be limited by this world or by ourselves; we wish to be free. But is this longing a wish upon a fallen star, never to be realized? Or does the story of Superman, in its own simple way, give us a glimpse of a promise that will be fulfilled? As limited creatures, we are drawn to the unlimited God who will one day free us. Truly, in the real story of Jesus Christ, if we share in his cross and resurrection, we will one day *fly*.

For just a moment, Peter realized the dream of no longer being confined by the physical limits of this world when he walked on water. In this miracle, Christ was showing us a glimpse of our future resurrected glory, when all of material creation will bow to the will of God, and to those who are in communion with him. In the particular way that he walked on water, Peter also showed us the way for this dream to be fulfilled. Peter was able to walk on water only as long as he kept his gaze firmly fixed on Jesus Christ. With our eyes on the prize, we can fly from lowly earth to heavenly heights.

Fictional heroes are prophets in a way, for unbeknown to their admirers, they create receptivity to the greatest hero of all, who, in reality, defeated what Superman or Hercules, in make-believe, could not. As amazing as Superman's feats of strength are, he can only save people from a particular death. But death itself they will have to face *again* someday. He can only temporarily right a wrong. He can't make the wrongness of death into a right. He can save Lois from an untimely death, but not from death itself. He can protect a person's body from harm by averting a crashing train, but he can't protect that same body from aging and inevitably crashing in death. Looking at the omnipresence of sin, the destruction caused by evil, and the inevitability of death, humanity *is* a train wreck.

But the fall of humankind is not the end of our story; it was part of our beginning. With Jesus, we begin the flight of humankind.

Clark Kent is a fictional Superman, but he is not *the* Superman who can defeat our triple threat of sin, evil, and death. For this enemy, we had need of someone more than super. We needed to learn how to surrender and die. Since God does neither of these, he became human so that he could show us how to do it perfectly. Jesus Christ is incarnate God, God become human. Just as the prophet John the Baptist pointed the way to Jesus, the mythological heroes of this world, both real and fictional, can point the way to *the* true Superman. He is closer than we realize. To uncover his secret identity, we need only love our neighbor.

3

Amadeus

WE ARE BELOVED OF GOD.

Saul Zaentz Company / Orion Pictures (1984)

Producer	Saul Zaentz
Director	Milos Forman
Author of Screenplay	Peter Shaffer
Running Time	160 minutes

MAIN CHARACTERS

Wolfgang Amadeus Mozart	Tom Hulce
Antonio Salieri	F. Murray Abraham
Constanze Mozart	Elizabeth Berridge
Emperor Joseph II	Jeffrey Jones
Leopold Mozart	Roy Dotrice

How could something as beautiful as Mozart's classical music, which can elevate the human spirit and bring us closer to God, have caused such misery in the lives of human beings? How could a great blessing have become a curse? The story of *Amadeus* explains how. It is about two musical composers, Antonio Salieri and Wolfgang Amadeus Mozart, and how their lives end in tragedy. Although the characters and their relationship are completely fictionalized, *Amadeus* does follow the basic historical outline of Mozart's life. Born in 1756, Mozart was a child prodigy under his father's tutelage. He was hired as a chamber composer for Emperor Joseph II where he met a court composer of some merit named Antonio Salieri. He married Constanze Weber and struggled with ever-increasing debts until his death in 1791 at the age of 35. His mysterious and untimely death made Mozart an ideal historical character for a dramatic tragedy.

When the Greeks invented drama, they wrote two kinds of tragedies. A classical tragedy told the story of a person who falls by virtue of a "tragic flaw"—a weakness in his own character. A domestic tragedy told the story of a person who falls because of circumstances beyond his control. *Amadeus* contains both. Salieri is brought to ruin by his own tragic hubris and jealousy. Mozart is both the unwitting victim of Salieri's hatred and his own character flaws. At the story's conclusion, Salieri is insane and Mozart is buried in a pauper's grave. In a tragedy, there is no happy ending. This is doubly true of *Amadeus*. Tragedy offers a different kind of happiness, one not found in the pages of the story. But we can find happiness if, by unlocking the message of the story, we can understand where Salieri went wrong and avoid that tragic path in our own lives.

Like the sun to the planets of the solar system, God is the center of the human system. Human creatures can only find happiness when we are revolving around the Son. If we try to take ourselves out of our ordered position in the heavens, we cause our own misery; we make our own hell. Or to use a more appropriate analogy, God is the Conductor of the symphony of life, who has designed each of us to be an ordered, musical note in a major chord. To the extent that each of us plays our unique, individual note, we make the symphony of life that much more harmonious, that much more beautiful and joyful. If we resist the role we were designed to play, if we choose to play a different note, it can only be dissonant and sour. Then, we bring disharmony, disorder, and misery to ourselves and to others.

Pride is the sin of human beings desiring to be in the center, human beings desiring to be the conductor rather than a valued, integral note of the symphony. Pride comes before the Fall. The resulting disharmony is the great tragedy of human existence.

The tragedy in *Amadeus* centers on Antonio Salieri. Just as the rock opera *Jesus Christ Superstar* is more about Judas than it is Jesus, similarly, *Amadeus* is more about Salieri than it is Mozart. Salieri is the main character. A more practical title for the film might have been *Salieri's Confession,* for the story begins and ends in an insane asylum, where an aging Salieri confesses his sins and struggles with Mozart to a visiting priest. Most of the story takes the form of a flashback. Salieri, since childhood, had earnestly desired the gift of great musical composition. And it is his disordered desire that leads to his ruin:

> I would offer up secretly the proudest prayer a boy could think of: Lord, make me a great composer. Let me celebrate your glory through music and be celebrated myself. Make me famous throughout the world. Dear God, make me immortal. After I die let people speak my name forever with love for what I wrote. In return I will give you my chastity, my industry, my deepest humility, every hour of my life. Amen.

The problem with Salieri's childhood prayer is that he was bargaining with God rather than discerning God's will. Salieri was trying to establish a covenant with God. He was brokering a deal for his own immortality. But from a biblical perspective, it is God who establishes a covenant. He sets the terms, not us. In his mind and heart, Salieri had a disordered relationship with God. Despite the external forms of prayer, fasting, and supplication, Salieri devoutly desired God to do *his* will. Conversely, true humility desires *God's* will to be done. Even in his childhood, Salieri had sown the prideful seed of his own doom.

In his adulthood, Salieri continued to believe that God would answer his prayer. Using the talent God gave him, he rose to the position of court composer to the emperor of Austria. Success and status he had, to be sure, but Salieri had never composed heavenly music that would be the very "voice of God." God had answered Salieri's prayer. His answer was *no*. It was a bitter pill that Salieri refused to swallow. And to make it even more rancid, God had given the gift he so coveted to a most unlikely recipient.

Salieri had heard of the prodigy Mozart all his life. Mozart had written his first concerto at four, his first symphony at seven, and full-scale opera at twelve. When Mozart arrives in Vienna, the city of music, Salieri is expecting to meet a man of heroic virtue who would match his musical genius. Instead, Mozart is shockingly the opposite. In addition to being musically brilliant, Mozart is silly, childish, flamboyant, and arrogant, complete with a high-pitched laugh. He wears pink wigs and purple satin coats. "That was Mozart! That giggly, dirty creature I'd just seen crawling on the floor."

Salieri was not the only court official who was skeptical of Mozart at first, but most of their reservations were lost when they heard his music. For Salieri, the beauty of the sound was both exquisite and painful. "I was hearing the voice of God. And why? Why would God choose an obscene child to be his instrument? It was not to be believed." It was incomprehensible to Salieri that God would humble himself to work through Mozart and not him. In his pride, he saw himself as worthy and Mozart as worthless.

We have heard it asked of God, "Why do bad things happen to good people?" But Salieri's question to God is the opposite: "Why do very good things happen to bad people?" Tragically, Salieri does not include himself as one of the "bad" people. He perceives himself as "good" and worthy of God's grace; Mozart is "bad" and unworthy. But we are all "bad" in the sense that we are all sinners. None of us leads a morally perfect life that warrants the eternally perfect gift of everlasting life. Regardless, God dispenses his gift of salvation, his grace, to us anyway.

Salieri sees God's choice of Mozart to be his voice as scandalous. He cannot accept a God who would grace Mozart to such a degree. This is the mystery of grace—that God freely and unconditionally loves the sinner and the saint, the prince and the pauper, the rich and the poor. His mercy and love are beyond the kind of measured justice that Salieri had bargained for in his youth. God's love is a gift, not an award. A gift is something freely given. It cannot be earned. It reveals the generosity of the giver, not the greatness of the receiver. An award, on the other hand, is something earned. It represents a greatness achieved by the receiver.

In parables, Jesus warned us not to become Salieris. The elder son in the story of the prodigal son (Luke 15:11–32) becomes angry that his father has killed the fatted calf in celebration of the prodigal's return. Like Salieri, the elder son doesn't understand grace. In the story of the workers in the vineyard (Matt 20:1–16), those who toiled all day in the field are insulted that all the workers received the same pay, regardless of how long they worked. Like Salieri, they don't understand grace. From their self-exalted position, the elder son and workers are blind to their own blessings, and overly mindful of the blessings bestowed on those they have labeled as undeserving. Through these parables, Jesus was trying to tell us that none of us deserves God's love. Love is not bestowed on us because we are generous; it is bestowed on us because God is generous. But because he sees himself as having earned the gift given to Mozart, Salieri is scandalized by God's choice to bestow such talent on so unworthy a person. *Amadeus* is the story of the scandal of grace.

In his utter confusion, Salieri allows the deadly sin of envy to take hold of him. "God was singing through this little man to all the world, making my defeat more bitter with every passing bar." Envy is one of the seven deadly sins, all of which flow through the sin of pride. Once we have disordered ourselves above God, the essence of the sin of pride, the gifts God has given us become disordered as well. Disordered sexual attraction becomes lust. Disordered relaxation becomes sloth. Disordered anger becomes wrath. Disordered appetite becomes gluttony. Disordered satisfaction becomes greed.

Instead of being inspired by Mozart's musical genius, Salieri only feels envy, a disordered desire that resents a person's talents, status, or situation. Instead of taking inspiration from someone else's gifts, envy begrudges someone else's good fortune or goodness, and takes pleasure in depriving the person of his fortune. Or as Dante Alighieri better put it, envy is the "love of one's own good perverted to a desire to deprive other men of theirs."

Salieri can believe in God, but he is incapable of believing in a humble God, because Salieri does not know humility. Salieri was intelligent enough to recognize genius when he heard it, but not humble enough to accept where God chose to display it. Instead of using his encounter with Mozart as a lesson from God in humility, Salieri feels only humiliation. Envy of Mozart turns to hatred of him—and to hatred of the one who had most generously bestowed his love upon Mozart—God.

Since God does not obey Salieri's covenant, Salieri makes a pact with the devil. Addressing a crucifix that he had cast into the fireplace, Salieri brazenly shouts at God,

> From now on, we are enemies, you and I. Because you choose for your instrument a boastful, lustful, smutty, infantile boy and give me only the ability to recognize the incarnation, because you are unjust, unfair, unkind I will block you, I swear it. I will hinder and harm your creature on Earth as far as I am able. I will ruin your incarnation!

Being a man so well versed in the language of Christianity, Salieri's hatred has rendered him ignorant of how the first attempt to ruin the incarnation turned out. There is no death without resurrection. His plot may succeed, but his cause will inevitably fail. We cannot destroy what is good. Salieri's design is doomed from the start. It is wrong enough to blame God, but to attempt to defeat him is the beginning of spiritual death, which manifests itself in Salieri's insanity.

Salieri's mindset is evil and unstable for him, but it is lethal for an unsuspecting Mozart. Since God had not granted Salieri one magnificent piece of music, he would steal it from God's mouthpiece, Mozart. Though ignorant of his own flaws, Salieri is smart enough to see Mozart's weakness. What Salieri wanted most was the world's approval. What Mozart wanted most was his father's approval.

Disguising himself in a death mask identical to one Mozart's father had worn at a masquerade, Salieri poses as a paying customer requesting a requiem Mass for the dead. Mozart's flamboyance and excessiveness have already made his health fragile—working on composition by day, which paid little, and partying beyond his means throughout the night. Knowing that Mozart was estranged from his disapproving father prior to his death, Salieri pushes Mozart to the edge, emotionally and physically. He will work Mozart to death and steal for himself Mozart's requiem Mass written for his father.

> My plan was so simple that it terrified me. First, I must get the death mass, and then I, I must achieve his death. His funeral! Imagine it, all of Vienna there. Mozart's coffin, Mozart's little coffin in the middle, and then suddenly, in that silence, music! A divine music bursts out over them all. A great mass of death. Requiem Mass for Wolfgang Mozart, composed by his dear friend, Antonio Salieri! Oh what sublimity, what depth, what passion in the music! Salieri has been touched by God at last. And God is forced to listen! Powerless, powerless to stop it. I, for once in the end, laughing at him!

With masterful cunning, Salieri succeeds in hastening Mozart's death and his own damnation. Both are brought to tragedy. Mozart could not find a way to deal with his superabundant gift of music. Salieri could not find a way to deal with his lack of it.

Salieri accomplished Mozart's death, but he could not suppress the power of the gift that had come through Mozart's soul. When the film begins, we see an elderly Salieri lying on the ground, having cut his own throat. Perhaps, over the years, he had come to regret his treatment of Mozart? Far from it. In the end, we see that Salieri had not attempted suicide because he regretted what he did to Mozart, but because he realized that he had failed to defeat him. "[God] killed Mozart and kept me alive to torture—watching myself become extinct." Though Mozart's body was gone, his spirit was alive in his music, stronger than ever, and Salieri's music is all but forgotten. Even as Salieri was rushed through the streets to the hospital, a nearby ballroom was filled with people dancing to Mozart's music. God was still laughing at him. The years hadn't lessened his hatred for God or God's chosen musical prodigy. His dementia had only increased. Hatred does more damage to the vessel it is stored in than the object it is poured upon.

Although Salieri confesses to the priest, it is no sacramental confession, and he shows no repentance. He therefore can receive no absolution. With no absolution, there is no relief from his self-imposed exile. The film ends with Salieri still in the mental asylum, his wheelchair being carted down the hallway. In a final moment of irony, Salieri dispenses an absolution to his fellow patients that he refuses for himself. "I speak for all mediocrities in the world. I am their champion. I am their patron saint. I absolve you. I absolve you. I absolve you."

The triumph in the film is the one thing Salieri could not possess nor destroy—the music of Mozart. The music in *Amadeus* is almost like a character. The perfect harmony of notes within Mozart's music serves as a contrast to the disharmony in the lives of Salieri and Mozart. It is not merely in the background, but, rather, it is the foreground of the story. Each mood and situation in the film is matched to a selection from a Mozart sonata, requiem, concerto, opera, or symphony. The music of Mozart not only sets the tone for every scene, it often moves the story along, substituting for the dialogue, intonating the characters thoughts and feelings. Long after Mozart is gone, the music lives on. Music is the sign of resurrection in *Amadeus*. For this, the real Wolfgang Amadeus Mozart should have received best supporting actor.

We cannot know why particular good things happen to other people. If we attain the virtue of humility, it ought not to be a problem. Although we do not always understand the mind of God, humility gives us the wisdom to know that God's purpose is more important than our satisfaction. God will often ask us to subordinate our pleasure to make possible a greater joy. When God does bestow a gift on us, humility teaches us that it is given for enjoyment and ennoblement, not for earning a validation we already have.

Wolfgang Amadeus Mozart was aptly named. *Amadeus* in Latin, means *beloved of God*. Mozart was given the gift of music so that he might come to know God's love. Each and every human being is graced with different gifts for the same purpose: that we might come to know we are beloved of God and that we might find joy in loving God in return. We are "Amadeus."

4

Hoosiers

CHRISTIANITY IS A TEAM SPORT.

Hemdale Film Corporation (1986)

Producer	Carter DeHaven
Director	David Anspaugh
Author of Screenplay	Angelo Pizzo
Running Time	115 minutes

MAIN CHARACTERS

Coach Norman Dale	Gene Hackman
Myra Fleener	Barbara Hershey
Shooter	Dennis Hopper

THE TEAM

Jimmy	Maris Valainis
Strap	Scott Summers
Rade	Steve Hollar
Everett	David Neidorf
Merle	Kent Poole
Buddy	Brad Long
Ollie	Wade Schenck

Most people have never been to Milan, Indiana, or even heard of it. But in 1954, the Milan Indians did what no other small-town basketball team had ever done in Indiana sports history. They won the Indiana State High School Basketball Championship. They overcame adversity. They beat the odds. Their story became the basis of the 1986 film *Hoosiers,* which renamed them the Hickory Huskers. *Hoosiers* is the story of champions.

"This is all well and good," one might respond, "but what does *Hoosiers* basketball have to do with Christianity?" By way of analogy, *Hoosiers* has everything to do with Christianity. Consider, first, the parallels between basketball and Christianity.

Some sports evolve over time. Other sports enter onto the scene overnight, tracing their roots to a single individual. The game of basketball is an American invention. James Naismith invented the game in December 1891. Unlike the evolution of rugby to football, or cricket to baseball, basketball began with one man's creativity, with his vision of teamwork and community. A former candidate for the Presbyterian ministry, James Naismith was a physical education director at the YMCA in Springfield, Massachusetts. He knew that spiritual truths and moral teachings are not learned in a vacuum. A community was needed. He wanted a game to help teach Christian principles. He posted two peach baskets onto ten-foot high rails of the balcony-jogging track on either end of the gym, divided eighteen members of his class into two teams, and began the game by throwing up a soccer ball between the two men chosen as centers. One of the players, Frank Mahan, suggested the game be called "Naismith ball," but Naismith himself preferred "basketball." Basketball was born. The game's popularity spread from gym to gym, with spectators soon coming to watch. Today, basketball is second only to soccer in its universal appeal. It is a team game, played in driveways, public playgrounds, school gymnasiums, and huge arenas throughout the world.

Some religions evolved over time. Others trace their roots to a single individual. Such is the case with Christianity. Unlike the evolution of world religions such as Hinduism, Christianity began most profoundly with the resurrection on the first Easter Sunday around the year AD 33, with Jesus Christ being the fulfillment of the Judaic faith that had gone before him. Encounters with the risen Christ by those who came to love him inaugurated a new understanding of God and his kingdom. Christianity was born. Community had been fundamental to the earthly ministry of Jesus, because it was fundamental to Judaism. Consistent with his religious heritage as a Jew, Jesus' first public act after proclaiming the kingdom of God was to gather disciples. The "team concept" was there from the beginning. He sent them to teach in his name, giving them the authority to forgive sins and cast out evil spirits. He taught them how to pray. He gathered disciples from tax collector to religious zealot. They witnessed wondrous signs daily and endured a nightmare one Passover night. In fact, the last thing Jesus did before he died was to consecrate the bread and wine into his body and blood, saying, "Do this in remembrance of me" (Luke 22:19), thereby placing sacramental worship at the heart of the religious community even before his death. And when he revealed himself that first Easter morning, the good news of Christ spread. Today, Roman Catholicism alone is over one billion strong; add to that all other Christian faith communities, and it is clear that Christianity, a team enterprise, comprises the largest and most influential religion on the face of the earth.

Why the need to emphasize the team concept of Christianity? In the past, during times of more strict cultural mores, Christians tended to emphasize their personal relationship with Christ—what we call the "vertical dimension" of their religion—but to ignore the communal obligations and benefits that have always been a part of Christianity—the "horizontal" dimension. In Roman Catholicism, the Second Vatican Council redressed the balance, reminding us that we are saved not as individuals but as the people of God. Here is where sports can help. In sports such as basketball, Americans can easily see the significance of both individual and team.

If basketball can, indeed, be analogous to Christianity, then there is no film that makes the case better than *Hoosiers*. This is the story of Norman Dale, a former college coach for the Ithaca Warriors, who was so driven to win that in his anger, he struck one of his players. His "win-at-all-costs" mentality lost him his job, along with a lifetime ban from NCAA coaching. Disgraced, he went off to the Navy for eight years. But coaching was his destiny. He wanted one last chance. It came to him in the most unlikely of places—Hickory, Indiana.

Hickory was only a spot on a map. It had no skyscrapers or subways or French restaurants, but it did offer one thing for Norman Dale that no other town could offer: a chance to coach. At the local high school, the principal, Cletus, remembered Norman Dale from years earlier and offered him the coaching job. It came with suspicious townsfolk and a team of only seven boys from an enrollment of sixty-four, but it also came with forgiveness. "Your slate's clean here. We've got a job to do," Cletus assured. "It's gotta work out this time, or that's it for good," Norman replied.

Before he could dribble a basketball, Norman Dale was ushered into the local barbershop one evening to be measured up by the local basketball boosters. "This town doesn't like change much, so we thought we'd get together tonight and show you how we do things here." They filled Dale in on their expectations and told him how he would coach the team. He listened and finally said, "Gentlemen, it's been real nice talking to you. Goodnight." This would be his team. He would be the coach; he would set the tone; he would be the authority. He would not bend his coaching to suit the townspeople. He made his vision of the team clear to his players on their first day of practice:

> Basketball is a voluntary activity. It's not a requirement. If any of you don't want to be on the team, feel free to leave right now....My practices are not designed for your enjoyment....I've seen that you guys can shoot, but there's more to this game than just shooting. There's fundamentals and defense....Five players on the floor function as one single unit. Team. Team. Team. Right? No one more important than the other.

If the players were able to accept his authority and become a team, they could do together what they could not do as individuals: become champions.

Coach Dale's attitude echoes that of Christ himself. Although Jesus reached out to all—the rich and the poor, the weak and the powerful—he would not compromise his ministry in order to appease the Pharisees or win popularity from his disciples. This would be his team. He would be the coach; he would set the tone; he would be the authority. He made his vision clear to his disciples: "I ask not only on behalf of these, but also on behalf of those who will believe in me through their word, *that they may all be one*. As you, Father, are in me and I am in you, may they also be in us, so that the world may believe that you have sent me" (John 17:20–21, emphasis added).

Standing as one, we can mount a legitimate defense against evil in the world. A communion of saints can rival sin, for saints are merely sinners—revised and edited. With forgiveness at the forefront of our creed, we can begin again, like Coach Dale. United in creed, reborn in baptism, the whole of the Christian community is greater than the sum of its parts. Coach Dale's words at the basketball rally describe succinctly why we need the Christian community: "to see who we are and to see who we can be." Together, we can help each other attain a level of goodness and a degree of sanctity we could not achieve on our own. Each of us can then see who we are and who we can be. As adopted sons and daughters of God, Christ can make us champions.

Far more profound than any team analogy found in *Hoosiers,* Saint Paul understood the communal nature of faith in Jesus Christ:

> For in the one Spirit we were all baptized into one body—Jew or Greeks, slaves or free—and we were all made to drink of one Spirit....As it is, there are many members, yet one body....If one member suffers, all suffer together with it; if one member is honored, all rejoice together with it. Now you are the body of Christ and individually members of it. (1 Cor 12:13, 20, 26–27)

To assent to faith in Jesus is to become part of the mystical body of Christ. To surrender in faith to God the Father makes us all children of the same God. No longer solitary, we can live and act in solidarity.

There is spiritual power in this unity. We're stronger arm in arm and hand in hand. After fleeing Germany from Nazi oppression, Albert Einstein learned firsthand the value of how Christians united can be a force for greater goodness in the world:

> Being a lover of freedom, when the revolution came in Germany, I looked to the universities to defend it, knowing that they had always boasted of their devotion to the cause of truth; but, no, the universities immediately were silenced. Then I looked to the great editors of the newspapers whose flaming editorials in days gone by had proclaimed their love of freedom; but they, like the universities, were silenced in a few short weeks....Only the Church stood squarely across the path of Hitler's campaign for suppressing truth. I never had any special interest in the Church before, but now I feel a great affection and admiration because the Church alone has had the courage and persistence to stand for intellectual truth and moral freedom. I am forced thus to confess that what I once despised I now praise unreservedly.[3]

The Christian courage to fight evil gave Einstein a second chance at liberty. Christianity is the religion of second chances. Since we rebelled against God and caused our own misery, God became human to give us a second chance. With his leadership, we have won the victory, not by our skill but by his love. We need only to choose to be on his winning team.

Again, *Hoosiers* parallels Christianity in giving Norman Dale a second chance. But his second-chance opportunity is not an easy one.

Facing opposition from town boosters and players, the Hickory Huskers are, at first, far from being a winning team for Norman Dale. They lose their first game, playing with only four players. Their second defeat ends in a brawl. Their third defeat has Dale ejected from the game. Losing breeds dissent toward Dale. In particular, a fellow teacher, Myra Fleener, is suspicious of him. "A man your age comes to a place like this, he's either running away from something or he has nowhere else to go." She is also a mentor to Jimmy Chitwood, last year's standout player, a one-in-a-million star athlete. He had declined to play, having been upset by the death of the previous coach. Given Norman Dale's past monomania for winning, Myra has reason to be protective. But the coach is trying to change. When he does have a conversation with Jimmy Chitwood, he does not use the opportunity to recruit him.

> You know, in the ten years that I coached, I never met anyone who wanted to win as badly as I did. I'd do anything I had to do to increase my advantage. Anybody who tried to block my pursuit of that advantage, I would just push him out of the way. Didn't matter who they were or what they were doing. But that was then. You have a special talent—a gift. Not the school's, not the townspeople's, not the team's, not Myra Fleener's, not mine—it's yours—to do with what you choose. Because that is what I believe, I can tell you this. I don't care if you play on the team or not.

This is not to say that Coach Dale is an exemplary coach. He is stubborn and short-tempered. He is far from perfect, but he is trying. No religious leader, be it pope or patriarch, priest or minister, is perfect, either. Personal sinfulness, however, does not remove their responsibility to speak with authority on matters of faith and morals. When the Hickory boosters petition the school board for a referendum to determine whether Norman Dale will remain as coach, he does not relinquish his authority in order to appease them. At the town meeting, he says,

> I've made some mistakes, but they're mistakes I take full responsibility for. I was hired to teach the boys the game of basketball and I did that to the best of my ability. I apologize for nothing. You may not be pleased with the results, but I am. I'm very proud of these boys.

Coaches don't win games, players do. Just when it looks as if Norman Dale will be replaced, Jimmy Chitwood speaks up. He agrees to join the team, provided the coach stays. It sometimes takes a star player to pull the team to a higher level of perform- ance. Similarly, the dogmas and doctrines of any Christian faith cannot alone transform the hearts of people. They are only the game plan, so to speak. It takes flesh and blood saints, ordinary men and women living extraordinary lives, to move a community to a higher level of holiness. Like Jimmy Chitwood for the Hickory Huskers, Francis of Assisi reinvigorated the medieval church from the bottom up. Mother Teresa of Calcutta challenged twentieth- century Christians to do something beautiful for God. The more corrupt the times we live in, the more God graces us with saints to show the way.

Mindful of his own personal shortcomings that led him to Hickory, Norman Dale tries to give Shooter a second chance, just as he received a second chance. Shooter is the alcoholic father of Everett, one of Dale's players. Norman offers him a chance at assis- tant coach. He does not judge him, but he does judge his actions. Shooter must be clean-shaven and on time, but most importantly, he must be sober. "If I smell even a trace of liquor on your breath, you're finished. You're embarrassing your son." Norman Dale fol- lows in the footsteps of Jesus, who reached out to sinners, making moral judgments without making personal judgments. But Shooter's own son is skeptical. After class one day, Everett says, "Coach, what you doing with my Dad; I'm not seeing it. He's a drunk. He'll do something stupid." "When's the last time someone gave him a chance?" Dale asks. Everett replies, "He don't deserve a chance." All grace is undeserved; it is a free gift given by God.

Shooter becomes an assistant coach. Dale even goes so far as to get himself ejected from a game to give Shooter an opportunity to lead the team to victory. Faced with a last possession chance for victory, it's up to Shooter. With his son looking into his eyes, hop- ing that he will rise to the challenge, Shooter calls for the "picket fence." He sets up a wall of players as a screen, which frees Merle for the game-winning shot. For a moment, Shooter's son can be proud of him. "You did good, Pop, you did real good." Shooter can hold on to that moment.

Shooter's alcoholism eventually gets the best of him. The pressure of sobriety and coaching leads to a relapse. In his drunkenness, he goes onto the court in the sectional final and embarrasses himself and Everett. He is admitted to a hospital to detoxify. The coach visits him to offer encouragement. He never gives up on him. Everett also comes to visit his dad in the hospital. When Shooter apologizes to his son for his addiction, Everett says, "It don't matter, Dad. You're going to get better. Couple months from now when you get out of here, we're going to get a house. I love you, Dad." Now, Everett offers a second chance. The coach has taught by example, with Everett learning the lesson. Norman Dale has helped give them a fresh start.

With Jimmy, the team comes alive. Teamwork, attitude, and talent—all come together. Victory after victory, like each piston firing together, the team reaches the play-offs. Before the regional final against Linton, Coach Dale gives his locker-room pep talk. But instead of spouting a win-at-all-costs speech, he shows real insight into the nature of victory:

> There's a tradition in tournament play not to talk about the next step until you've climbed the one in front of you. I'm sure going to the state finals is beyond your wildest dreams, so let's just keep it there for a while. If you put your effort and concentration into playing to your potential, to be the best that you can be, I don't care what the scoreboard says at the end of the game, in my book we're gonna be winners.

Champions are not recorded on a scoreboard alone, but in the heart of every person who strives for greatness.

The Huskers battle to the end. With one player injured, Strap, the preacher's son, enters the game. "God wants you on the floor," the coach says. When another player fouls out, Ollie, the team's equipment manager, is the last player available. Then, with seconds remaining, the Huskers down by one point, Ollie—the smallest and least skilled player—is put on the foul line to make two shots. Strap holds on to Ollie's hand in prayer during the last time-out. "Make it a good one, Strap," Coach Dale injects. With hundreds of people screaming, and the team's season on the line, Ollie makes them both. Hickory goes to the state finals for the first time ever. No small town team had ever come as far, and they made it on the shoulders of their smallest player. Hickory climbs into the state championship. Each contributes what he can. No player is without value.

The heaven of high school basketball is the state championship. At the huge Butler Field House in Indianapolis, the Huskers are teamed against the defending state champions—South Bend Central. Central's front-line players are comparable giants at six-foot plus. With big players from a big-enrollment school of 2,800, South Bend Central is the Goliath of Indiana high school basketball. Before the game, Coach Dale says with calm sincerity, "I want to thank you for the last few months. It's been very special to me. I love you, guys." Their pregame prayer is an appropriate one: "And David put his hand in the bag and took out a stone and slung it. And it struck the Philistine on the head and he fell to the ground. Amen."

The game of basketball is a drama, as is life. We love miracle stories in sports because we long for them in life. For Hickory, the miracle happens. Coming back from an enormous deficit in the fourth period, with time for one last attempt at a game-winning shot, Jimmy Chitwood comes through—nothing but net.

Because team sports have become so much a part of our cultural landscape, few would deny the benefits of team competition when the game is properly played. Could you imagine someone saying, "I like Michael Jordan, but I don't think you need to be part of a team to play basketball. I play basketball on my own"? And yet, to the extent that religion is marginalized in America, we may hear those who have assented to belief in Jesus make statements like, "I believe in Jesus, but I don't think I need to be part of a church in order to be Christian. I practice religion on my own." But the believer cannot separate Christ from his church anymore than, to use Christ's own image, a vine can be separated from its branches. Christ is the vine; we are the branches.

An honest examination of the scriptures reveals that we cannot separate Jesus from his community of believers any more than we could separate Paul McCartney from the story of the Beatles, or Hootie from his Blowfish. The group is part of the experience.

It is through the testimony of the early church that we even know of Jesus. We come to know him according to Matthew, Mark, Luke, and John, who were disciples themselves. Before there was the New Testament, there was first the early church that lived the story, wrote the story, and gave acceptance to the orthodox version of the story. Any person today who assents to belief in Jesus has also unwittingly assented to the early church as a reliable and authoritative source for Jesus.

Organized Christian religion takes the ideal of Jesus and makes it real. It becomes a daily flesh and blood activity, with demands on our time, patience, and conscience, as does family. Any team sport asks for a real commitment and real work. It is not an endeavor for the spiritually lazy. Playing basketball on a team is a lot different from watching it on the sidelines. Being part of a team requires practice, hard work, and personal sacrifice. Being a member of a Christian community requires communal prayer, worship, and service. No scientist who is serious about his craft, even an Einstein, would separate himself from the scientific community or a laboratory. Although he could do some rudimentary observations without reading Galileo or using a microscope, they would be meager indeed. By isolating himself, he would lose the benefit of learning from the mistakes already made in the past, and learning from the achievements within the present community. That would be imprudent. No lover of basketball would reject being part of an organized league in order to further hone his skills. Yet, directed against Christianity, we continue to hear, "Spirituality is good but religion is unnecessary. Church is for the weak, unthinking sheep of the world."

Perhaps the detractors of organized religion are closer to the truth than they realize. They are right. Religion *is* for the weak.

Who among us has conquered sin on his or her own? Who among us can do battle with evil single-handedly? Who among us can defeat death? Who among us is not weak? Humanity is a chain that is only as strong as our weakest link. Paradoxically, it is the recognition of weakness that is true strength, as it is for recovering alcoholics in AA. Christians do not only stand united; we kneel united. The little lamb, David, did not battle the giant wolf, Goliath, alone. The Lord was his shepherd, and a rock his defense. But David only won the battle; he needed faithful Israelites to win the war. They won together.

The Hickory Huskers make for an inspirational story about second chances, forgiveness, and reaching out to sinners. Possessing the talent, they were in need of discipline and guidance from a great coach. *Hoosiers* is a celebration of what teamwork is meant to accomplish. The small-town boys defeated the big-city giants. Together, the basketball band of brothers experienced victory.

If games can teach us anything, we might draw a lesson from the Huskers. As we do battle with the giants of sin and evil, both around us and within us, we are in need of a good shepherd. Jesus is the foundation upon which Christianity is built. He is the rock that can pierce any sinful barrier. Together, we band of brothers and sisters in Christ can experience the ultimate victory.

5

Rain Man

STRONG IS THE BOND OF BROTHERS.

Mirage Entertainment / United Artists (1988)

Producer	Mark Johnson
Director	Barry Levinson
Authors of Screenplay	Barry Morrow/Ronald Bass
Running Time	133 minutes

MAIN CHARACTERS

Charlie Babbitt	Tom Cruise
Raymond Babbitt	Dustin Hoffman
Susanna	Valeria Golino
Dr. Bruner	Gerald R. Molen

Rain Man is a film with virtually no romance. No action sequences. No slapstick comedy. No car chases. No fist fights. No sharp, witty dialogue. No shoot-outs. No courtroom drama. No special effects. No surprise happy ending. *Rain Man* should be a washout. Yet it was a box-office success, with movie lines that became part of popular culture, and won Academy Awards for Best Actor, Best Director, Best Original Screenplay, and Best Picture of 1988. *Rain Man* is a journey saga, and the secret of its success lies in the relationship between the two main characters, Charlie and Raymond. brothers

Charlie Babbitt is a handicapped man. It's hard to put a handle on his disorder—arrogance, selfishness, anger, materialism, or workaholism—take your pick. His mother died when he was a child, and he's estranged from his father. He's a man without family, a self-centered Donald Trump wannabe who is as driven as the upscale cars he sells. All he has left of his family is the memory of an imaginary childhood friend he called "Rain Man." To be more precise about his handicap, Charlie carries within him the poison of entitlement—the attitude that life owes him something. The deep emotional bruises resulting from it have led Charlie to distance himself, first from his father, and then from anyone else who might try to get close to him. To be *most* precise, Charlie's greatest handicap is that he is oblivious to even having a handicap. The poster boy of 1980s materialism, Charlie wants everything but has no one. Or at least he thought he had no one, until one day he discovers an inheritance no balance sheet can estimate—a brother.

As the film begins, high-end car salesman Charlie Babbitt receives a phone call informing him that customs officials are holding his shipment of four Lamborghinis at dock, due to possible EPA violations. Charlie's reaction: animated passion—which includes motivated fast-talk and gamesmanship that temporarily save his small Los Angeles outfit from losing its desperately needed customers to a competitor. The next day, uptight Charlie Babbitt is on the road to a Palm Springs vacation with his girlfriend, Susanna, when he receives a phone call that his father has just passed away. Charlie's reaction: stoic indifference—no tears, no shock, not even anger. Cars he is passionate about, not his father.

Charlie travels with Susanna back to his hometown of Cincinnati, Ohio, where he learns that his father, Sinclair Babbitt, has bequeathed him a mint-condition 1949 Roadmaster convertible and some rosebushes. The entire remaining three-million-dollar estate is left to a trustee, who is holding the money on behalf of a beneficiary. The trustee is Dr. Bruner of Wallbrook, an institution for the mentally handicapped. The beneficiary, Charlie learns to his surprise, is the older brother he never knew he had—Raymond.

Raymond Babbitt has autism, a mysterious brain disorder that permanently damages a person's ability to communicate and interact with others. As Dr. Bruner explains Raymond's autism to Charlie:

> It means there's a disorder that impairs his sensory input and how it's processed. Raymond has a problem communicating and learning. He can't even express himself or probably understand his own emotions in a traditional way. There are dangers everywhere for Raymond. Routines, rituals—it's all he has to protect himself. It's the way he acts: eats, sleeps, uses the bathroom, walks, talks, everything. Any break from this routine and it's terrifying.

All of this goes in one ear and out the other for Charlie, who is more mindful of the money he has lost than the brother he has gained.

It may be that at Wallbrook "everybody loves Raymond," but it is not the case with Charlie. For him, brother Raymond is a means to a financial end; leverage on a three-million-dollar payoff that he feels is rightfully his. Spiteful of his father's decision, Charlie kidnaps Raymond from Wallbrook to take him to Los Angeles, where he can begin a custody battle for Raymond and thereby get access to his share of the inheritance. Because Raymond is terrified of flying, "Airline travel's very dangerous. Flying is very dangerous," Charlie is forced to drive the six-day cross-country journey in the 1949 Roadmaster. When Susanna discovers Charlie's less-than-filial intentions, she leaves him. "You use me; you use Raymond; you use everybody."

Charlie callously takes Raymond away from the familiarity on which he so desperately relies, never considering the effect the change might have on him. So Raymond persistently searches for ritual consistency in order to cope. Such is the nature of his disorder. "Gotta get my boxer shorts at K-Mart...Definitely watch TV but lights out at eleven...Maple syrup is supposed to be on the table before the pancakes...One minute to Wapner (*The People's Court* TV show)...." Raymond flummoxes insensitive Charlie.

Incapable of any depth in ordinary relationships, Charlie is even more bewildered by the behavior of mentally challenged Raymond.

Raymond clings to things like TV shows and notebooks because of a disorder in his brain. Charlie clings to things like vintage cars and inheritance money because of a disorder in his heart. Who is the more handicapped?

Wallbrook is genuinely interested in Raymond's well-being, but Charlie is interested in Charlie's well-being. As their journey begins, Charlie reacts to Raymond's disability by ignoring it until it drives him crazy. He then tries to reason with Raymond like he is negotiating with a client. When Raymond gets nervous, he recites the classic Abbott and Costello comedy routine "Who's on First." Oblivious to the nature of Raymond's disorder, Charlie tries to explain it away:

> Ray, you're never going to solve it. It's not a riddle because Who *is* on first base. That's the joke, Ray, it's comedy. But when you do it you're not funny. You're like the comedy team of Abbott and Abbott.

But it is Raymond's autism that is a riddle Charlie can't solve or accept. And through the first part of their journey, his frustration inevitably turns to anger. "Put the phone book down, stop acting like an idiot and go to sleep....You know what I think, Ray? I think this autism is a bunch of sh--. Because you can't tell me that you're not in there somewhere!...Don't act like a f---ing retard!" Charlie acts as if Raymond's disorder can be fixed, like a Lamborghini in need of a tune-up. He is asking for flexibility from a person who is incapable of it, which is like asking a man without legs to tap dance. Thus, Charlie puts himself in his own self-made purgatory of frustration. He doesn't accept Raymond for who he is, and acceptance is the prerequisite for love, and love is the only way to real happiness.

Charlie acts as if mentally challenged persons have the power to change themselves from within and be cured with a little discipline and a book on the power of positive thinking. And he isn't alone.

Similar attitudes are held by so many regarding the mentally ill. In *Rain Man,* Charlie finds it preferable to criticize his brother's autism rather than turn the criticism onto his own narcissistic behavior.

But a hostile attitude toward the disabled is nothing new. Heresies never die; they can only be buried alive, until they resurface. Jesus encountered a similar heresy centuries ago within a Jewish culture, which believed the disease or misfortune that befell individuals was the result of their own sin, or the sin of their family. Consequently, they were shunned, which only added guilt and loneliness to their disease. They needed so desperately the saving grace that Jesus had to offer—the good news that God loved them unconditionally, that he had not forsaken them. They needed that truth to penetrate their hearts to relieve them of their shame and to touch the hearts of others so that they might be treated as worthy of love.

Christ never valued people on the basis of what they could do, only for who they were—a son or daughter of the Father, made in his image and likeness. The danger implicit in Charlie's materialist mentality, one of the competing American cultural attitudes, is that once we define our humanity functionally rather than personally, then the result is either the marginalization or elimination of the unborn, the elderly, the crippled, the terminally ill, the mentally handicapped—any category of persons who do not tangibly produce. Reduced to less-than-human status, they get pitied, avoided, ignored, feared, condescended to, or removed.

Just as there is hope for America, there is hope for Charlie, stuck as the sole caretaker of his brother. In the day-to-day, no frills hard work of real love, Charlie slowly begins to show glimpses of an attitude change. It starts when he discovers that being disabled doesn't mean the absence of ability, particularly, when he learns of Raymond's unique gift for memorization and numerical computations. For example, when a box of toothpicks spills onto a restaurant floor, Raymond instantaneously calculates the correct number of fallen toothpicks as eighty-two. He can multiply three hundred twelve times one hundred twenty-three as quickly as we multiply four times four. He can memorize exact names and addresses from a phone book. Autistic savants often possess amazingly advanced musical, artistic, or numeric skills. Charlie begins to see Raymond not merely as disabled, but as able to do what others cannot.

One of the subtle cinematic themes set against the backdrop of the cross-country trek is nostalgic America. Forced to drive only on back roads (Raymond becomes frightened of interstate highways after seeing an accident), the odd couple stays at roadside motels, listens to oldies tunes on the radio, eats at local diners, speaks about past baseball greats, and drives in a vintage car across the desolate but beautiful American landscape. Both cinematography and sound track evoke memories in the viewer of those long summer vacation trips that were never easy, but left a lasting impression of the value of family. It is as if director Barry Levinson is contrasting a slower-paced, nostalgic America that took the time for family, to the fast-paced, 1980s, individualistic lifestyle that Charlie embodies.

But the real thaw in Charlie's glacierlike demeanor occurs one evening in a hotel room, when Raymond utters the phrase, "funny rain man." The words freeze Charlie in his tracks, and he makes an immediate connection with his past. "You? You're the rain man?" Charlie asks in bewilderment. Charlie realizes that as a toddler, he tried to say "Raymond" but it came out "rain man." Moments later, when Charlie turns on the bathtub water, Raymond gets hysterical. Charlie is able to piece together from Raymond the reason why he was sent to Wallbrook Institute—Raymond had come near to burning his baby brother with scalding water in the bathtub. With Raymond gone, Charlie had only the memory of what became an imaginary friend. All Raymond had left was a picture of Charlie and himself, which he guarded with care.

For the first time, Charlie begins to really look at Raymond—not as a pawn in a money deal, not as an autistic puzzle—but as his brother. To borrow the language of philosopher Martin Buber, Charlie moves from an "I-it" relationship, one of person to object, to an "I-thou" relationship, one of person to person. He no longer sees Raymond as the three-million-dollar man but as the rain man. He stops trying to change Raymond into what he is not capable of becoming. He begins to assume the responsibility for the care of his brother, and in the process Charlie regains his brother. He is no longer alone. Nowhere is this better visually illustrated than when the two are in a Las Vegas hotel suite, set against a window backdrop of all the glittering night-lights of the Vegas strip, fluorescent monuments to gambling and material riches...and Charlie patiently teaches his brother how to dance.

Having stormed out of his father's life at the age of eighteen, furious that his father would not let him drive the 1949 Roadmaster that he felt he had earned, Charlie's attitude that life owed him something had left him alone, abrasive, and insolated. Now, by learning how to love his brother, Charlie slowly moves from a toxic sense of entitlement to a healthy sense of responsibility. Psychiatrist Victor Frankl realized the vital importance of this attitude shift while a prisoner in Auschwitz and wrote of it in his memoir, *Man's Search for Meaning*:

> What was really needed was a fundamental change in our attitude toward life. We had to learn ourselves and, furthermore, we had to teach the despairing men, that *it did not really matter what we expected from life, but rather what life expected from us.* We need to stop asking about the meaning of life, and instead to think of ourselves as those who were being questioned by life—daily and hourly. Our answer must consist, not in talk and meditation, but in right action and in right conduct. Life ultimately means taking the responsibility to find the right answers to its problems and to fulfill those tasks which it constantly sets for each individual.[4]

When Charlie arrives in Los Angeles at the completion of his journey, we get the sense that a new journey has begun. His spiritual change is subtle and gradual, which lends to the believability of the story. (He still teaches Raymond to count cards in Vegas to make fast money.) Charlie never completes his extreme spiritual makeover. But his newfound attitude does lead him to reconnect with his girlfriend Susanna and apologize for his insensitivity and aloofness—and we get the definite feeling that "I'm sorry" had previously never been a popular part of Charlie's vocabulary. Charlie begins to value the happiness that comes from family ties.

During the journey, Charlie had hoped to change Raymond, but it is Charlie who is most significantly changed for the better. When Dr. Bruner arrives in Los Angeles for the pretrial psychological evaluation, he offers Charlie $250,000 just to walk out of Raymond's life and allow him to return to Wallbrook. Charlie can't accept. "It's not about the money anymore," he says to Dr. Bruner. At the evaluation, Charlie tries to explain his change of heart:

> I had a father I hardly knew, a mother I didn't know at all. I found out a few days ago I have a brother I want to be with and I'm supposed to give him up?

> You have to understand that when we started out together that he was only my brother in name. And then…then this morning we had pancakes. You see we…I…made a connection.

Seeing his brother get more and more nervous with questions from the psychologist, Charlie realizes what an enormous toll a legal trial would take on Raymond. "No more questions," he promises Raymond. Charlie comes to realize that he is not capable of protecting Raymond all the time, and that the Wallbrook Institute is not a cold, heartless cuckoo's nest. They are better suited to take care of Raymond. Charlie's letting go is not a failure to love; it is an expression of his love.

Some might think that a movie about a cross-country trip involving a mentally challenged man and his brother, a movie that never mentions God or Jesus, faith or salvation, is hardly a source of Christian insight. Albeit hidden, Jesus is very much a part of *Rain Man*. Possessing far greater authority and wisdom than I do to reflect on this mystery is Jean Vanier, a man who has spent a lifetime learning from the mentally challenged. In 1964, Vanier invited two men with developmental disabilities, Raphael Simi and Philippe

Seux, to live with him in community. He called the community L'Arche, a name referring to Noah's ark, and the movement has spread from its original home in France to the four corners of the earth. Jean Vanier wrote:

> It's a sad secret of Jesus that he's hidden in a very special way in the poor, and in the broken, and in the suffering. Whatever you do to the least of my brethren, the smallest of my brethren, the most broken of my brethren, you've done unto me.

> The mystery is that Jesus is hidden in the poorest and the weakest. But then also the mystery that he is hidden in the poverty of my own being, that he is hidden in my poverty....There again, there is fear in our hearts, because if this is true, if Jesus is hidden in the hearts of the smallest and the weakest and the suffering, if he's hidden in my poverty, well then its a revolution.

> And of course this revolution means a completely disordering [sic] of the order. It's the breaking down of the fortress of prejudice, it's bringing humanity into one, it's breaking down the walls, and of course all these walls that have been created are the walls of security. It's the security of prejudice: I know who I am and I'm powerful. But in some way Jesus is breaking all this down to bring us into the insecurity of communion, the insecurity of love, the insecurity where God is present and calling us all forth.[5]

Once Charlie acknowledges the intrinsic value of his brother hidden in the poverty of his handicap, he begins to acknowledge the poverty of spirit within himself. We are all handicapped; some just hide it better than others.

In the film's final scene, Charlie brings Raymond to the railroad station to return with Dr. Bruner to Wallbrook. Good brother that he now is, he supplies Raymond with his daily necessities of cheese balls, apple juice, and notebooks for the journey. Before Raymond departs, Charlie confesses, "I like having you for my brother. I like having you for my big brother."

Charlie promises Raymond that he will visit Wallbrook in two weeks, and the audience can be confident that he means it. Because Raymond is incapable of expressing the complexity of sentiment that Charlie conveys, we are left to wonder how the experience has affected Raymond. Given that Raymond never forgot about his brother Charlie, that he held on to his picture for all those years, that he showed a quiet comfort with Charlie by the film's end—it is a safe bet to conclude that Raymond is happier with the bond as well, content in his own way to be close to his brother again. Previously almost incapable of reaching out to touch others, Raymond reacts to Charlie's parting words by placing his head gently on Charlie's shoulder.

As the credits scroll, we see various black-and-white photos that Raymond had taken throughout the trip—offering the audience one last opportunity to see life through Raymond's very special eyes. The mentally challenged are neither angels nor demons; they are human beings. But the cross that they carry can generate within them an attitude to live and love simply in a world that the average person can overcomplicate. I have seen them trust and love with a freedom that the greatest of intellects would envy. They remain a sacrament of love to the world.

Rain Man is not an overly sentimental story. Charlie doesn't become a wonderful person at the end, as does Phil Connors in *Groundhog Day* (discussed in chapter 11), nor is Raymond the recipient of a miraculous healing, as Jarius's daughter is. There is no ending scene of Charlie running after the train, catching it and embracing his brother and taking him home forever. There is no final breakthrough for Raymond where he can now function normally. The limitations placed on the ending are a result of the real limitations inherent in the characters. Screenwriters Ronald Bass and Barry Morrow respected the realities present in a relationship with an autistic person.

In the end, Charlie is content that a love connection has been made, and I think the audience should be too. *Rain Man* is a poignant movie about the healing power of love. It ends not in the full flowering of love but the germination of love—the love between two brothers, one prodigal, one elder—and we have witnessed only the beginning. Strong is the bond of brothers.

6

Indiana Jones and the Last Crusade

LIFE IS A DIVINE ADVENTURE.

LucasFilm Ltd. / Paramount Pictures (1989)

Producer	Robert Watts
Director	Steven Spielberg
Authors of Screenplay	George Lucas/Jeffrey Boam
Running Time	127 minutes

MAIN CHARACTERS

Dr. Henry "Indiana" Jones, Jr.	Harrison Ford
Professor Henry Jones, Sr.	Sean Connery
Dr. Marcus Brody	Denholm Elliott
Dr. Elsa Schneider	Alison Doody
Walter Donovan	Julian Glover

At the outset of the Middle Ages, church and state in the West had woven themselves into an all-encompassing entity known as Christendom. Inevitably, legend and folklore began to surround the life of Christ. One example of this was the legend of the quest for the Holy Grail. The word *grail* is derived from *graal,* a word still used in France to refer to a wide-mouthed cup. The peasants and nobility were interested not in any ordinary cup, but in *the cup* used by Jesus Christ at the Last Supper. By the thirteenth century, the search for the cup of Christ and the story of King Arthur's Camelot had been interwoven. In one of the most popular versions of the Holy Grail story, written in the late Middle Ages by Sir Thomas Malory in his book *Morte d'Arthur,* the cup awaits only the one most worthy of the prize. Sir Lancelot, because of his adulterous relationship with Queen Guinevere, only sees the Holy Grail in a dream. Sir Perceval, having committed but one sin, is permitted to see it in visions. Only Sir Galahad, who is pure in heart and deed, is graced by God to look upon the Holy Grail itself and enter a mystical union with God.

The search for the Holy Grail and other such stories embodied the hopes of the common men and women of Christendom. They sought to live a life of holiness, with a vision of God, symbolized by the sacred cup, as the ultimate reward. Galahad represented the ideal Christian, for Jesus Christ was the focus of his life's journey. The nobility of his quest was as much a reward as was the vision of the Holy Grail he was granted at its end. Christ was both the source and culmination of an honorable life.

Today, the search for the actual cup Christ used at the Last Supper is the stuff of legend. As such, it is ideal source material for *Indiana Jones and the Last Crusade.* The third film of the 1980s Indiana Jones trilogy, the *Last Crusade* is the story of Indiana Jones, played with humor and bravado by Harrison Ford, who must save his father and the cup from Nazi treachery.

Indiana Jones is a great adventure story. Made in tribute to the movie serials of the 1940s, its hero has become one of America's most popular screen characters, ever since *Raiders of the Lost Ark* premiered in 1981. Additionally, in the process of enjoying Indiana's adventure of a lifetime, we can realize what he lives out in his stories: life is an adventure! We are able to see his heroic adventure from a different vantage point than we do our own life adventure. From it, the nature of the adventure story has much to teach us.

Imagine you are in a movie theater with an ice cold Pepsi in one hand and a large buttered popcorn in the other. You are ready to enjoy a movie from the chronicles of Indiana Jones—

archaeologist and adventurer extraordinaire. The theater darkens, the familiar theme music starts, and the fun begins.

But to be obtuse for a moment, what fun? Looking at this from Indiana Jones's point of view, *fun* wouldn't be the first word he would use to describe his situation. Throughout his adventures, he is attacked by a lion, surrounded in a vat of snakes, beaten by thugs, entombed with rats, almost torn up by a propeller blade, tied up to be burned alive, fired at from the air by machine guns, dragged by tanks—all in a day's work for him. This is not exactly the dream vacation. And yet, an Indiana Jones movie *is* a vacation to watch—a film fantasy of fun. Why don't the misery and mayhem within the story cause us sadness?

The answer is as near as the closest child. Any kid knows that we enjoy the pain and peril of Indiana Jones because we know that it is all going to work out in the end. No matter how impossible the odds, or how heavy the burden he bears, Indiana will prevail. The happy ending will show the struggle to be well worth it. We don't wonder *whether* there will be a happy ending, only *how* it's going to occur. We are fairly certain of the outcome. Indiana may not be, but we are. The characters on the screen do not know what we know; to them belong the toil and the success. They must hope against hope for a happy ending that we know is assured. In a sense, we in the audience are like "God." We are certain that the beginning, middle, and end will all weave together to create a cinematic tapestry. Our certainty of the happy ending gives us a serenity that Indiana does not have. Omniscience has its benefits.

But in the film of life, we are not spectators, removed from the ebb and flow. We are characters within an unfinished story, steeped in struggle and uncertain of the next act. We are asked to perform a quintessential role that God has directed us to play. Being *in* the picture, we can't *see* the big picture. So when we blame God for allowing sin and suffering, we are assuming a divine perspective that we simply do not have. We do not have the vantage point to be a critic, only an actor.

This wisdom, that human beings simply lack the vantage point to see what God sees, is essentially the Old Testament insight into the problem of human suffering. We see this exemplified in God's answer to Job, when Job questions the sufferings that have been given to him, and, in effect, to all of us. Rather than answer Job's question, God remains God. Refusing to be the one on trial, God turns the tables and interrogates Job. It is Job's pride that is put on trial:

> Where were you when I laid the foundation of the earth?
> Tell me, if you have understanding. Who determined its
> measurements—surely you know! (Job 38:4–5)

Like Job, when we assume the capacity to make judgments of God, we have entered a "temple of doom," for the divine wisdom we seek is not accessible to humankind. It remains the prerogative of God whose methods are designed for all of salvation history. It is no wonder that we can't make sense of everything God does. There is no madness to God's method; our prideful assumptions of superiority are the only madness. And our confusion is just that— our confusion. Not to understand someone's purpose does not make that person confused. We cannot use a modicum of human justice to judge the Creator, who is divine justice himself. We are not in a position to see the big picture, only to play our role in it.

God, on the other hand, does see the big picture. God created the picture. God is the paramount author, the executive producer, and the director of the universal studio. Unlike the screenplays of human beings, God's screenplay allows the actors to ad-lib. Because the divine nature is love, God created us free so that we would have the capacity to love as well. Free will is the necessary precondition for love. Therefore, God will not eliminate evil. If he does, he eliminates free will as well. If God takes away free will, he takes away the possibility of love, and God won't do that. In the divine wisdom, God has allowed the characters to shape their part within the story, even if they script personal tragedies. Yet despite our bad plot twists, God has not relinquished executive control. The master script ultimately flows from his hand. God can take our tragic choices and move them toward triumphs. In Psalm 46 God tells us, "*Be still,* and know that I am God!" (v. 10; emphasis added). God has earned that trust. God knows what he is doing.

When we sit back in a movie theater and enjoy the perils of Dr. Henry Jones, Jr., we can learn as well as be entertained. In one important way, the art of Indiana Jones has imitated life. Simply stated: Life is a trilogy. No one installment of any movie trilogy tells the whole story. The audience, as well as the characters, needs to complete the trilogy in order fully to grasp its meaning. But in the story of life, no one reading these words has concluded the trilogy. Yet by faith, we do know God's basic story line:

Episode One: The Mother's Womb. We live in physical darkness and breathe in water. We are surrounded by our mother's love, but are unable to see her face to face. We cannot walk or talk. We grow and become more than what we were. Life in this early world ends in a cliffhanger—a sometimes traumatic labor and birth— where we are transported into another world. And this ending turns out to be only a new beginning.

Episode Two: The Father's Womb. We live in spiritual darkness and breathe the air. We are surrounded by God the Father's love, but are unable to see God face to face. We learn to walk and talk. We grow and become more than what we were. This life, too, ends in a cliffhanger—a sometimes traumatic death and dying—where we are transported into another world. And this ending turns out to be only a new beginning.

Episode Three: Real Life Begins. We live in the full light of Christ and breathe the Holy Spirit. We are permeated by the love of God, and through our beatific vision we can see clearly in others and ourselves what was once cloudy. We learn fully to walk in faith and live in love. There is no cliffhanger ending to this world. We grow to become what God had intended us to be. It is a happy ending that never ends.

It is only in *Episode Three* that we find out how the first two episodes were merely prologues to the real story. Earthly life is a rough draft compared to the finished masterpiece of eternal life. The final episode takes all the random events and mysterious turns of the first two episodes and turns them into epiphanies. It makes sense of what seemed senseless. From an eternal point of view, all calamities will be calmed. All adversity will be reversed. Any judgments made by us against God in *Episode Two* were done either in ignorance or arrogance, because they were made without experiencing or considering *Episode Three*.

But how can we, still characters in *Episode Two,* have any knowledge of *Episode Three?* Enter the New Testament insight into the problem of human suffering. Unlike *Indiana Jones,* Christian faith offers a concrete historical sign of the happy ending in life's trilogy. Not aloof or removed from our sufferings, the playwright entered into the play. He became the main character, embracing joy and enduring pain, even to the point of death on the cross. But even happier still, he rose to show us that we can transcend the sufferings we face. The resurrection of Jesus Christ gives us a glimpse of the ending of the story in the middle, a sneak preview of *Episode Three*. For his ultimate contribution to the "last crusade," Jesus clearly has won best supporting actor, for he supported us when we could not support ourselves.

Although much of *Indiana Jones and the Last Crusade* is simply fun action sequences amid the magic and miracle of the search for the Holy Grail, the final dramatic scene provides an even more valuable treasure for us—Christian wisdom.

At the Canyon of the Crescent Moon, Indiana, Henry Jones, Sr., and Marcus Brody discover the cave of the Three Knights of the Holy Grail. Aided by the Nazis, Walter Donovan and Dr. Schneider capture the gallant trio. Donovan believes the ancient legend that promised that whoever drinks from the cup would achieve immortality. He wants it all to himself. But Donovan knows that finding the secret location is not enough. Three lethal tests await anyone who would seek to find the Holy Grail. Being a coward himself, Donovan aims his gun at Indiana. "Shooting me won't get you anywhere," Indiana says. "You know something, Dr. Jones, you're absolutely right." Donovan turns and fires a lethal bullet into Henry Jones, Sr.

Indiana finds himself faced with a decision of the heart. Seeing his father mortally wounded, he must decide whether to try to retrieve the Holy Grail that could miraculously save his father's life. "You can't save him when you're dead. The healing power of the Grail is the only thing that can save your father now. It's time to ask yourself what you believe," says the villainous Donovan. The choice is Indiana's. The scientist in him might doubt the truth of legend, but the son in him selects faith. He chooses to believe in the reality of a power mightier than bullets. In the hope of saving his father's life, he chooses to risk his own and go for the Holy Grail.

Bigger tests await him. Guided by his father's notebook that contains clues he had gathered from sacred traditional sources, Indiana walks through a gauntlet of three tests. The first test had warned, "Only the penitent man will pass." As he walks, he realizes that penitence means humility, and a humble person would kneel. Kneeling, he avoids a sword to his throat. He then reaches a narrow path that has each stone marked by different letters. The second test had warned, "Only in the footsteps of God will ye proceed." In Christ, we come to know his Father by name. Solving the riddle, Indiana surmises that the footsteps must literally spell out the name of God. With some difficulty, he spells out the word *Jehovah.* Two down, one to go.

After passing the first two tests, Indiana finds himself on the edge of a precipice, separated from the other side by a huge, bottomless chasm. He must walk "the path of God." According to the notebook, for the man of faith, "only in a leap from the lion's head, will he prove his worth." But it is humanly impossible to jump to the other side. To his eyes, a step off would mean certain death. "It's a leap of faith," Indiana says. His father lies dying. He can only quietly say to his son, "You must believe, boy. You must believe." Indiana stands silent to gather courage, places his hand on his heart, closes his eyes for a moment, and then…steps off the edge. Amazingly, he doesn't fall. Once he takes the leap of faith, from that vantage point he sees a stone path that was unseen from the cliff itself. It is only visible after the leap is taken.) His faith is vindicated. Indiana makes it to the other side, where he is eventually able to save his father's life. But without "the leap of faith," a term popularized by the philosopher Sören Kierkegaard,[6] he would not have found the salvation he sought.

Faith comes down to a personal decision to resign control. With hands over our hearts, in fear and trembling, we surrender ourselves to God. The leap of faith is the essence of what it means to be religious. It may seem absurd by human standards that limit themselves to material and ephemeral conditions, yet it is wisdom to God and wisdom for us. And just like Indiana Jones, once we take the leap of total self-surrender to God, only then will we cast a religious light on the meaning and mystery of human existence. In faith we will understand.

Having passed the three tests, Indiana meets the legendary Grail Knight who has miraculously guarded the cup for seven hundred years. As it turns out, the cup is also a test itself, as is the life of the man who made it holy. It is a test that the Nazi mentality cannot comprehend. The Nazis seek to exploit the cup's power of immortality, which Henry Jones, Sr., had been wary of from the start. As he had reminded Indiana earlier, "The quest for the Grail is not archaeology; it's a race against evil. If it is captured by the Nazis, the armies of darkness will march all over the face of the earth. Do you understand me?" Heroes understand what the cowardly cannot. When Dr. Elsa Schneider, in league with the Nazis, chooses a cup for her benefactor, the traitorous Walter Donovan, she chooses the most elaborate. Donovan takes of its water to claim eternal life for himself. He does not heed the Grail Knights' warning: "Choose wisely, for as the true Grail will bring you life, the false Grail will take it from you." Donovan's pride brings him immediate death. "He chose…poorly," the Grail Knight observes.

But Indiana does not seek fame or fortune from the Holy Grail, only its power to heal his dying father. With many cups to choose from, Indiana does not pick the one decorated with gold and precious gems. He understands that the cup would reflect the life of Jesus. "This is the cup of a carpenter," he says, as he reaches for the most simple and humble of cups. Exactly. The wise understand that the secret of immortality lies in humility. "You chose...wisely." Humility had saved Indiana's life in the first test. Now, with the Holy Grail's miraculous properties, his humble choice leads to the healing of his father.

Seeing the Holy Grail as a trophy and not as a relic, Dr. Schneider ignores the Grail Knight's warning not to remove the cup from the confines of the cave. Dangling over a bottomless pit, she reaches for the cup instead of giving her other hand to Indiana. She falls to her death. Similarly, when the edge of the precipice gives way, Indiana finds himself dangling over the edge, with only his father's grip keeping him alive. For a moment he, too, reaches for the priceless artifact. But it is his father who tells him, "Indiana, Indiana, let it go." The life and death adventure has taught Professor Jones a valuable truth. Having spent a lifetime pursuing the sacred relic, Professor Jones realizes now that his son is far more precious. Persons are more intrinsically valuable than things, even sacred things. As he admits to Indiana:

> "Elsa never really believed in the Grail. She thought she'd found a prize."
> "And what did you find, Dad?"
> "Me? Illumination."

✮ Illumination of the mind and heart toward God is what the Holy Grail was meant to signify all along.

Marcus Brody had said, "The search for the Grail is the search for the divine in all of us." To find the divine and God's real promise of immortality, we do not have to travel to the Canyon of the Crescent Moon. We need only to find within ourselves an attitude of humility, which illuminates the value of every human being around us. God is found when our ego is lost, in heroic humility, in the surrender of faith.

We can be enlightened by Indiana's adventure, as we take on the adventure of our lifetime, which only sets the stage for the adventure beyond this world. Each of us is a character in an adventure of epic proportion. There are no small roles, only small actors. We can take God's direction scripted by his word and play our part in the greatest story ever told, surrendering in faith; or we can depart from the script and become a lost raider of his ark of the covenant. The chronicles of our lives are now playing. The adventure continues.

7

Field of Dreams

WITH GOD ALL THINGS ARE POSSIBLE.

Gordon Company Universal Pictures (1989)

Producers	Charles and Lawrence Gordon
Director	Phil Alden Robinson
Author of Screenplay	Phil Alden Robinson
Running Time	106 minutes

MAIN CHARACTERS

Ray Kinsella	Kevin Costner
Shoeless Joe Jackson	Ray Liotta
Terrance Mann	James Earl Jones
Moonlight Graham	Burt Lancaster
The Voice	Himself

In 1994, five years after *Field of Dreams* premiered, Becky DuBuisson had a dream one night. When she awoke, she felt compelled to be at the field of dreams located near Dubuque, Iowa, at midnight on New Year's Eve eating a hot dog and drinking a root beer. She did just that. Seven months later, she married Dan Lansing, the owner of the white farmhouse and baseball field featured in the film.

"People will come, Ray," Terrance Mann says to Ray Kinsella at a key dramatic moment in the story, "People will most definitely come." As it turns out, the fictional Terrance Mann spoke a truth that even screenwriter Phil Alden Robinson could not fully fathom when he first put those words to paper. Ever since the release of *Field of Dreams,* year after year people *have* come. As if on a pilgrimage to Mecca, people continue to visit the quiet baseball field hidden in a cornfield. It is not an abandoned movie set; it has become almost a shrine, drawing those touched by the magic of the film.

Why all the interest? The answer lies in unlocking the meaning within the story of *Field of Dreams.* There is something about the film that strikes a powerful chord of truth. *Field of Dreams* is not about baseball, not about dreams, not about family, and not about heaven. It is about all these things, and more.

Field of Dreams is the story of Ray Kinsella, a 1960s flower child turned Iowa farmer, who, one day while working in his cornfield, hears a mysterious voice whisper to him, "If you build it, he will come." Ray comes to realize that the voice is asking something extraordinary of him. Just as Noah had once built an ark on dry land, Ray must build a baseball field in the middle of his corn crop, so that Shoeless Joe Jackson can come back from the dead and play again the game he once loved.

This extraordinary premise has a popular appeal for the ordinary individual, despite the fact that there is no earthly magic that can make the premise of *Field of Dreams* realistic or believable. But there is a heavenly magician who can. Although the film never mentions him, although Robinson may not have been aware of it, there is an interpretation as clear as the movie advertised on the theater Ray sees in Chisholm, Minnesota—*The Godfather.* Only God could alter linear time and allow Ray to enter the past of 1974. Only God could release Shoeless Joe Jackson from his purgatory of exile and reunite him with baseball. Only God could make a deceased Moonlight Graham alive and young again. Only God could reconcile a father with his prodigal son. "Is this heaven?" Shoeless Joe asks. For those of us with the capacity to take the leap of faith, so beautifully demonstrated by Ray Kinsella from the start of the film, the answer is a wonderful yes. God is the maker of fields of dreams. Follow his voice, and God will lead us to healing that is our deepest longing, beyond our wildest dreams.

Field of Dreams is unique in that the main character is never seen. Even more central than the character of Ray Kinsella, played effortlessly by actor Kevin Costner, is the character of "the voice." The voice has connected the dots of human events in a way that Ray cannot yet see. Ray Kinsella has to believe—not in the magic, as the screenwriter cautiously calls it, but in the magician behind it. The voice cannot be a real objective thing, as we are asked to accept, unless there is a real source to the voice. Voices are attached to persons. Connect the last dot, the one that Ray never consciously connects, and we have a powerful religious film. See the voice as the voice of God, and the film becomes more than magic—it becomes meaningful.

Field of Dreams is likely to be classified as a dramatic fantasy, yet it is far more realistic than most of the gritty dramas that Hollywood offers, if we see it through the eyes of faith. Interpreted in this light, the film is the story of a journey whose itinerary has been planned by an unseen God. And just as the Greek gods sent Odysseus on a ten-year journey, Ray is asked to navigate a voyage of faith.

From the start, Ray does not ask for scientific proof to verify the existence of the voice, nor does he ignore the voice or try to explain it away psychologically. He simply believes. He moves beyond doubt, trusts his intuition, and is willing to play the fool. Ray easily walks to the first "base" of faith that every individual must reach: he accepts that there is an invisible reality that surrounds and interfaces with the visible. Ray goes where the atheist and agnostic refuse to go. He accepts the reality of God and builds the field. "I have just created something totally illogical," Ray says, as he gazes out on the completed baseball field. It may seem illogical, but what is foolishness to a human being is wisdom to God. There is a logical purpose to the field that neither Ray nor the viewer can see at that point in the story, but in time the purpose will be revealed.

But there is more to salvation than mere belief, for the possibility of Ray and others being healed of their deepest pain hinges on whether Ray can "go the distance" and reach home, through the three "bases" of faith exemplified in Christianity.

There is a brief but poignant scene after Ray first builds the field and waits for Shoeless Joe Jackson to arrive. It shows him in his home at Christmas, looking out on the field covered with snow, still waiting. Ray waits months for the miracle promised in his vision to occur. There is a powerful message here. God acts at a time of his own choosing, not when we want him to act. God is in control; we are not.

And occur it does. Miraculously, Shoeless Joe Jackson returns to play the game he loves. And just when Ray is finally vindicated, content to have answered God's call, God asks even more of him. God wants more from Ray than one strange task. He must reach the second "base" of authentic faith—discipleship. Like the disciples who were called to abandon their nets and respond to the voice of Christ, Ray must follow where the voice takes him, no matter how improbable that path may seem. He travels to Boston and Chisholm to ease the pain of both the reclusive writer Terrance Mann and the noble doctor Moonlight Graham, who never got to bat in the major leagues. Reaching second base asks for selflessness. Ray is not told to ease his own pain; he is told to ease someone else's pain. He, and we as well, must act to help others without asking, "What's in it for me?"

But God does not want mere acknowledgment or obedience. God wants us to be ultimately happy, to be healed of our deepest pain. In order for that to happen, we have to open ourselves up to the Source of happiness—God. God wants more from Ray than building a field; more even than sending him across the country to find Terrance Mann and Moonlight Graham. What God wants is even more frightening than that. God does not want Ray to only follow his words; God wants Ray.

Finally, at a dramatic moment in the story, Ray must reach the third and final "base" to become a true knight of faith. From there, God will lead him home. Ray is asked to choose between the visible and invisible reality. He has to choose which is most important. It is not enough for him to believe and follow the voice; finally, he must go the distance and surrender himself over to this other reality, and trust that somehow it will make all things right.

On the one side, representing the spiritual realm, is Terrance Mann, who offers Ray a prophetic promise:

> Ray, people will come. They'll come to Iowa for reasons they can't even fathom. They'll turn up your driveway not knowing for sure why they're doing it. They'll arrive at your door as innocent as children, longing for the past. Of course, we won't mind if you look around, you'll say. It's only $20 per person. They'll pass over the money without even thinking about it: for it's money they have and peace they lack....This field, this game: it's a part of our past, Ray. It reminds us of all that once was good and could be again. Oh, people will come Ray. People will most definitely come.

Terrance's words about baseball are but a metaphor for a deeper longing we have all experienced. The longing may come *through* baseball, but it is not *from* baseball. The longing is for heaven. Heaven is the Elysian field of God.

On the other side of temptation, representing those who see only the material conditions of our existence, is Ray's brother-in-law, Mark. He has eyes but does not see what Ray is able to see with his heart. How many times have we missed the reality of God's presence because our eyes were blurred by the speed of our frantic lives? In the story Mark is not so much a villain as a nonbeliever. He operates from a limited perspective, believing that what he sees with his eyes is all that there is. Mark is a man of the world in the worst sense of the term. "Look Ray, it's time to put away your fantasies and come back to reality," Mark declares, after he walks across the baseball field, oblivious to the reality of the players around him. He is articulating the modern antireligious sentiment: religion is a comfortable illusion that people should keep to themselves. When it comes to money matters or politics, we need to grow up, put our little faith-games aside, and deal with the real world. Mark articulates the poison of secularism—a worldview devoid of God.

People of faith today echo Ray's response to Mark, "It's not a fantasy, Mark; it's real." God is not a product of our minds; our minds are a product of God. God is not an opinion; God is ultimately real. It is Mark's illusory worldview that keeps us blind and in our pain.

"Where is God?" people cry out with self-righteous indignation. "Where is God with all the suffering in the world?" But if God seems distant, who moved? Terrance Mann is given the same mystical vision at Fenway Park that Ray is given, yet he chooses at first to ignore it. How many of us have been contacted by God, yet missed the message? How many times have we drowned out the voice of God in the cacophony that is our hectic and frazzled lives? Elijah heard the voice of God not in an earthquake, but in a whispering sound. So does Ray Kinsella. God is heard in solitude and simplicity.

With God, the main character, removed from the story of life, the plot gets lost along the way. The jaded and cynical see religious dreams as pipe dreams that never come true. Selfish desire seems a safer bet. The fear that holds us at bay is the fear that it is all too good to be true, that the world couldn't have such a happy ending, that we are setting ourselves up for a fall. But we already have fallen. We have no place to go but up. If we are drowning, we should not refuse a lifesaver for fear it might sink as well. Without it, we will sink for sure. Without God, we have already sunk.

It is not that our dreams are too wild; it is that they are not wild enough. Self-centered dreams of pleasure or power, in addition to being destructive, are also too timid and fragile. They are the dreams of animals, not the dreams of beings made in the image and likeness of the Divinity. We are meant for more joy than we dare admit. Worldly cynicism and agnosticism are products of our fear. But the longing inside us cannot be fully quelled. The longing in our hearts remains, despite how persistently our intellect tries to suppress it.

Ray sits on the wooden bleacher, deciding whether to give the deed of his land over to his worldly brother-in-law, Mark, who in his ignorance plans on destroying the "worthless" field. Which will it be? Which reality is most important: the invisible or the visible; the City of God or the City of Humanity; the temporary or the eternal? Jesus had already laid out the choice. "No slave can serve two masters; for a slave will either hate the one and love the other, or be devoted to the one and despise the other. You cannot serve God and wealth" (Luke 16:13). The music builds as Mark warns him, "You will lose everything, Ray; you will be evicted." Precisely. Ray must lose his life in order to save it.

What Ray Kinsella doesn't realize at that moment is that the fulfillment of his deepest dreams and those of his companions hinges on his decision. Finally, Ray goes the distance. He chooses to trust God, believing that people will come, somehow drawn to the heavenly magic of the field, even though he doesn't entirely understand the master plan.

In our moment of trust and surrender, our dreams become subsumed into the will of God. Then and only then, the improbable becomes possible. For Ray Kinsella, having gone the distance, healing is now at hand.

Field of Dreams reveals the handiwork of God. Follow God's voice and God will lead each of us to healing. The key characters in the film can find salvation if they surrender to the path revealed by the voice of God. The root word in the term *salvation* is *salve,* which refers to healing. Heaven is the culmination of healing, where we become who we are meant to be. Though God's way may not always be easy to follow, it always leads us to the same destination sought by any baseball player—home.

Terrance Mann is a character who had at one time followed the voice, but the unwelcome baggage of the world had become too much of a burden and he gave up. He abandoned life and, with it, his writing. As he admits to Ray in Boston, "I wish I had your passion, Ray. Misguided though it may be, it is still a passion. I used to feel that way about things." But God offers him a way back to his passion through Ray's request for help. Joining Ray's quest, and arriving at the field of dreams, Terrance is invited by Shoeless Joe to enter the cornfield, the entrance and exit used by the heavenly baseball players. In other words, Terrance is offered a trip to heaven. When Ray asks him if he is going to write about the experience, he says, "It's what I do, Ray." Exactly. Once again, he is the journalist he was born to be. He had reported on life; now, he can report on life beyond life. God had led him to where he needed to be. Terrance Mann's pain is eased.

Witnessing the offer Terrance is given for a "journey beyond a lifetime," Ray finally shows his human weakness. He wants to go instead of Terrance. He gets selfish. He wants the fulfillment of dreams promised to another. But Shoeless Joe, the voice of heavenly wisdom, bluntly replies to Ray, "You weren't invited....Is that why you did this Ray, for you? I think you better stay." Ray is put in his place, with the fulfillment of his dreams closer than he knows.

Moonlight Graham's pain is less obvious and less profound, but all pain will be vanquished by heaven's light. Graham knew that medicine was his best destiny, and he never strayed from that true calling his entire life. When Ray laments Graham's lost opportunity to bat in the major leagues, Graham gently corrects him, "Son, if I had only been a doctor for five minutes, now that would have been a tragedy." Ironically, when a transformed Graham is finally given his chance to play with the "boys of summer" on the field of dreams, he doesn't hit a double, but rather a sacrifice—a fitting play for a man whose life had been devoted to sacrifice for others.

The voice had not led Moonlight Graham to the field so that he might continue to play the game; he is there to find out if he had the talent to play baseball with the best of the best. It was a question he was never allowed to answer during his lifetime. But life is much greater than any earthly lifetime. The field of dreams provides the setting for Moonlight Graham to be granted his answer. When faced with the choice to be doctor or a player yet again on the field of dreams, Moonlight again becomes Doc Graham and cures an ailing Karen. His choice to become a doctor is vindicated. But before his exit, he is given the confirmation he sought. "Hey rookie," Shoeless Joe Jackson says to Moonlight Graham, "you were good." Perfect. That is what he came to find out. Moonlight Graham's dream is realized.

John Kinsella, Ray's father, like his hero Shoeless Joe, longed to play again the game he loved, which age and circumstance had taken from him during his earthly life. He had lost the game, but more importantly, he had lost his son. But on God's heavenly field, he is given his youth and the game of his youth. And most profoundly of all, he is given a greater blessing. A prodigal father reconnects with his son.

For Shoeless Joe, John Kinsella, and Moonlight Graham, the fact that their dreams do not come true in their lifetime does not mean that they do not come true. Faith reveals, like the lines of a baseball field, that life is open-ended with no time limits. As the teacher Morrie Schwartz reminded us as he was dying of Lou Gehrig's disease, "death ends a life, not a relationship." Death is the end of the first chapter, not of the whole story.

Ray Kinsella sacrificed for the good of Shoeless Joe, Terrance Mann, and Moonlight Graham. In following God, he has led others to joy. In doing so, he has ensured his own reward. Like a good curve ball, the story takes an unexpected turn. The servant shall be served. Baseball had been something that Ray had once held in common with his father. But in the arrogance of his youth, he had insulted John Kinsella and left him. His father died before Ray could right his most regretful wrong. Now, the mystical baseball field provides the setting for a reunion much more important than any game.

Ray beholds his Dad, alive again, full of resurrected youth and enthusiasm for life. Ray is given what will heal his heart, as a grateful prodigal son reconnects with his father, just as we shall reconnect with God our Father one day.

The climactic ending is touching and powerful, because for a brief moment the story touches the deepest part of our heart, where we long for the truth that is visualized before us on the silver screen to be true in real life. We long to be reconciled with those from whom we are estranged. We long for death not to be the end. We want to feel their love once more. We want to be able to say "I love you" to those who most matter but are now gone. And every male in the audience knows that that is exactly what Ray

Kinsella has said to his father. Men tend to say it without saying it. Men often speak in deeds, fearful of the effect the words might have. But every male knows. "Dad...do you want to have a catch?" is "I love you."

Ray asks his father, "Is there a heaven?" "Oh yes," he replies with a smile, "heaven is the place where dreams come true." Ray stands next to his beloved father and looks upon his wife and child, and knows in the marrow of his being that he is experiencing a glimpse of heaven, which all along was as close as his own back-yard.

What brings a tear to our eye in vicariously experiencing Ray's deepest dream of reconciling with his father is that we secretly hope that the same can happen to us. We long for that to be, even after the lights in the cinema are turned back on and we walk out into our daily lives. And that longing, triggered in the story explains much of its appeal. Visitors touch the field in Iowa because they were touched by the story.

Kevin Costner called *Field of Dreams,* "our generation's *It's a Wonderful Life.*" If the happy ending offered in the story reflects something true of real life, then life truly *is* wonderful. Secure in Jesus' promise, Christianity dares to make the bold claim that our deepest dream has come true.

Happiness will be on that most glorious of days, when each of us will turn to our heavenly Father, wanting finally to give him the love that is due him, and ask, "...do you want to have a catch?" Reunion. Reconciliation. God and you. When pain is finally resurrected into joy. When all that was broken is restored. When all that should be...is. Heaven is a field of dreams come true. Safe at home.

Until that moment, we live a life filled with glimpses of a glory yet to come. God will come when we construct a soul that will let him in. If you build it, he will come.

8

Beauty and the Beast

BELIEVING IS SEEING.

Walt Disney Pictures / Buena Vista Pictures (1991)

Producer	Don Hahn
Directors	Gary Trousdale, Kirk Wise
Author of Screenplay	Roger Allers (script supervisor)
Running Time	84 minutes

MAIN VOCAL CHARACTERS

Belle	Paige O'Hara
The Beast	Robby Benson
Gaston	Richard White
Mrs. Potts	Angela Lansbury
Lumiere	Jerry Orbach
Cogsworth	David Ogden Stiers
Maurice	Rex Everhart

In the 1930s, Walt Disney dreamed of doing with cartoon art what had never been done before—creating a full-length animated feature film. But what story should he tell? For source material, he wisely looked to fairy tales. He banked his entire financial future on the animated film *Snow White and the Seven Dwarfs*, which premiered in 1937 to fabulous success and critical acclaim. The film became a significant benchmark in movie history, and its success propelled Walt and his studio into a golden era of movie animation, which gave the world film classics like *Pinocchio, Sleeping Beauty, Cinderella,* and *Peter Pan.*

Walt Disney understood the treasure buried within fairy tales—stories tested by time, surviving because they testify to basic elemental truths. *Sleeping Beauty* proclaims that love is stronger than death. *Jack and the Beanstalk* teaches that prideful giants need to be toppled. *Rumplestiltskin* warns us that evil covets the innocent. *Little Red Riding Hood* cautions adults to beware the wolves of the world. *The Frog Prince* notes the princely nobility within every person. Journeying through a fairy tale's magical world, we recover fundamental truths that get lost in day-to-day familiarity and routine. Fairy tales are a wake-up call from the dull haze of complacency, to see all things in a fresh, new light.

Even before Walt Disney had decided on *Snow White* for his first feature film, he was interested in bringing to life the fairy tale *Beauty and the Beast,* and he did considerable work on it in the 1930s and again in the 1950s. Problems in developing a satisfactory second act, however, led Walt to shelve the project—only for it to be reclaimed in the late 1980s by his nephew, Roy, then vice-president of Disney, who was interested in trying to bring the animated studio back to its glory days. Having achieved popular and critical praise in 1989 with an animated version of Hans Christian Andersen's *The Little Mermaid,* Disney Studios settled on a classic fairy tale as the perfect follow-up project. *Beauty and the Beast*'s time had finally come.

Beauty and the Beast is truly "a tale as old as time," having its ancient roots in Greece, India, and Africa. But the best-known version of the story is French, written in 1756 by aristocrat Madame Jean Marie La France de Beaumond, which Disney Studios used as the basis for their own version. The story begins as the inverse of *Cinderella.* In the original story, Cinderella, being humble of heart, shows kindness to an old woman who later reveals herself to be Cinderella's fairy godmother. She rewards Cinderella's kindness by raising her from rags to riches; her humility is exalted. Conversely, the prince in *Beauty and the Beast* is prideful of heart, and he spurns an old woman who turns out to be an enchantress. She punishes his shallowness by making what was attractive hideous; his exaltedness is humbled.

Fresh from their success on *The Little Mermaid,* writer and lyricist Howard Ashman and composer Alan Menken chose a traditional Broadway musical style in which the songs would further the plot line as well as entertain and develop the characters. Just as Walt had surrounded Snow White with seven lovable and comical dwarfs, executive producer Howard Ashman added a new twist to the story by turning inanimate objects that were part of the beast's castle into characters, to bring both comedy and perspective to the story. Like Snow White's dwarfs or Cinderella's mice friends, they witness the drama between Beauty and the beast from the audience's point of view and enhance much of what the audience is experiencing.

The Disney-spun fairy tale begins from the beast's viewpoint, as pictures etched in stained-glass windows combine with narration to establish the rules of enchantment. Once upon a time...there was a beastly prince who rejected a haggard old beggar woman and her offer of a rose in exchange for a night of warm shelter. Having warned the prince not to be deceived by appearances and that beauty is found within, the beggar woman revealed herself to be an enchantress. Seeing no love in his heart,

> She transformed him into a hideous beast and placed a powerful spell on the castle and all who lived there. Ashamed of his monstrous form, the beast concealed himself inside his castle with a magic mirror as his only window to the outside world. The rose she had offered was truly an enchanted rose, which would bloom until his 21st year. If he could learn to love another and earn her love in return, by the time the last petal fell, the spell would be broken. If not, he would be doomed to remain a beast for all time. As the years passed, he fell into despair and lost all hope. For who could ever learn to love a beast?

Howard Ashman's creative addition of new characters helped to flesh out the story beyond the fairy tale's narrow focus on just two characters. In doing so, he unwittingly added a great theological insight: the beast's sin has repercussions beyond himself. Servants become objects and castle statuary takes the shape of monsters. The crew and castle are "fallen" just as Adam and Eve's original sin caused a resultant "fall" throughout all of creation. Individual acts have communal consequences.

In *Beauty and the Beast,* as in *Cinderella,* the enchantment is a transformation of appearance, not of substance. The prince's identity substantively remains the same. Therefore, for the prince-turned-beast, the enchantress's spell wasn't just a metamorphosis but also a revelation, revealing the ugliness that was already there, forcing it to be seen by the prince's own eyes. The "eyes" are a dominant visual theme that runs throughout Disney's *Beauty and the Beast.* With the enchantment, the beast could no longer escape the truth that was once concealed within, nor could he control his anger over what he had become. Anger turned inward is depression; it is the road toward hopelessness.

What remains the same for the beast before and after the enchantment, in addition to his inability to love, is his lack of faith. Faith is the capacity to see beneath the surface *of* reality to see what is essential *in* reality. (What is most essential is God, the ultimate object of faith, but this not an explicit topic in this story.) Since love and faith are two sides of the same coin, the prince's lack of love hinders his capacity for faith. For the beast, *seeing is believing.* And just as he is blind to the ugliness within himself before the enchantment, he lives in blindness to any beauty that remains within after the spell. The voice of the beast, Robby Benson, best describes his character as a "tortured soul." The beast lives alone and in the shadows where his eyes do not have to see what he has become; his castle is a dark reflection of the prison his life has become. Time and hope are running out, as petals fall off the rose like sand falling through an hourglass. As the narrator wonders, "Who could ever learn to love a beast?"

The answer to the narrator's question is—a human being—but not just any human being. It would have to be a human being with beautiful eyes that could see beneath the surface, eyes that could see beauty inside a beast—the eyes of faith. As said by the brilliant Greek philosopher Anonymous, "Faith gives us real eyes to realize where the real lies." Enter our leading lady—Belle, named for the French word for *beauty*.

The animators intentionally drew Belle *not* to be the most comely of Disney leading animated ladies, to place the emphasis on her beauty within, the depth of her heart and soul. Perhaps not the fairest one of all to a mirror on the wall, she exemplifies what true beauty is—she possesses a virtuous heart. Belle is attractive but not conscious of her feminine beauty, which makes her even more beautiful. She is selfless and fiercely attentive to her eccentric father, Maurice. Her happiness doesn't depend on finding a man. She reads books, particularly fairy tales. (What wonderful irony: a fairy-tale heroine who reads fairy tales and wishes to be in one.) She is intelligent and wishes for adventure. She is the quintessential heroine—heroic because she demonstrates love and relies on her gift of faith to see what is really real. In another fairy tale of sorts, *The Little Prince,* by Antoine de Saint-Exupéry, the fox teaches the little prince, "It is only with the heart that one can see rightly, what is essential is invisible to the eye." Belle can see rightly. For Belle, *believing is seeing,* because her faith allows her to *see* essential beauty revealed by deeds and not by looks, and that guides how she responds to the world. As Blaise Pascal wrote in *Pensées,* "Faith declares what the senses do not see, but not contrary to what they see. It is above them, not contrary to them." Belle lives the creed that "beauty is found within," and she is the embodiment of hope for the beast.

Despite her spiritual qualities, or perhaps because of them, the shallow townsfolk find her to be peculiar and odd (as is often the plight of a real-life saint). She doesn't fit in with her superficial surroundings, as she wonders out loud in her opening song, "There must be more than this provincial life."

There is. Fairy-tale adventure awaits our future princess. Master fantasist J. R. R. Tolkien defines fairy story as: "the adventures of men [and women] in the Perilous Realm." By "Perilous Realm," Tolkien refers to a magical world filled with possibility and danger, where choice determines destiny. In a fairy tale, only the virtuous decision brings about the happy ending. In the case of *Beauty and the Beast,* it is for the beast to choose to love; it is for Belle to choose whether she can love what appears unlovable.

All good fairy tales need an antagonist. In *Beauty and the Beast*, it is the stereotypical and entertaining Gaston, who is able to be both comic relief and villain. Gaston is as the beast once was. If the beast is hideous on the outside but still carries a heart of gold beneath layers of fur, Gaston is his opposite—ruggedly handsome (and inadvertently funny) on the outside and rotting on the inside. He makes Narcissus look considerate. "I use antlers in all of my decorating!" Gaston proudly sings of himself. Charming as long as he gets his way, brawn with little brain, Gaston is a self-absorbed town superman who leaps over tall blondes in a single bound. Accustomed to getting what he wants, he covets a trophy he can't have—Belle—the only beauty in town who can see beyond his biceps.

Both Gaston and the beast prey on Belle's love for her father to manipulate her. Gaston plots to have Maurice thrown in an insane asylum if Belle does not agree to marry him. The beast binds her by her word to stay at the castle in exchange for her imprisoned father, who had trespassed into the castle when lost. But love cannot be coerced, and Belle is too genuine to be deceived.

The dynamic between Belle and the beast changes when the beast protects her from a pack of vicious wolves. Belle has the opportunity to leave, but freely chooses to stay and tend to the beast's wounds. Only then does their relationship become one of equals, and romantic love becomes possible. Freedom is the nutrient soil needed for the rose of love to grow.

As Belle and the beast begin to relate as friends, we see the beast gradually change externally to mark the internal spark of his returning humanity—"just a little change, small to say the least," as the love theme intonates. His clothing gradually becomes more civilized. He walks more upright, less with the prowl of an animal. His eyes bespeak moments of weakness and vulnerability. He listens to his servants instead of bullying them with growls. He offers his library of bounteous books as a gift to Belle and treats her like a lady. He dances gracefully with her in a chandelier-lit ballroom (a scene that marks Disney's first use of computer animation, used to give a sense of camera movement to the background, which matches the flow of their dance). Conversely, as Gaston's plans are thwarted, he becomes more animal-like in demeanor, more villainous, and eventually outright evil.

Both Belle and the beast experience some of the sensations that go along with the spark of love. "There may be something there that wasn't there before," they both acknowledge in a duet. As love begins to clear away the fog of his selfish misery, the beast realizes that Belle must be allowed to leave if she wishes. Through the magic mirror that he has offered her, Belle sees her father in danger and must tend to him. The beast grants her freedom. Knowing that the enchanted rose has almost shed all its petals, the beast chooses Belle's happiness over escape from his enchanted prison. He has reached the first condition of breaking the spell— he has learned to love another, for love is to will the good of another. Unbeknown to him, his princely sacrifice has made possible his salvation. All that is left for the spell to be broken is for the beast to be loved in return.

This sets the stage for the happy ending. Of all of the characteristics of a fairy tale, there is none more essential than the "happy ending." As Tolkien notes in his essay *On Fairy Stories*,

> Far more important is the Consolation of the Happy Ending. Almost I would venture to assert that all complete fairy-stories must have it. At least I would say that Tragedy is the true form of Drama, its highest function; but the opposite is true of Fairy-story. Since we do not appear to possess a word that expresses this opposite— I will call it *Eucatastrophe*. The *eucatastrophic* tale is the true form of the fairy-tale, and its highest function.

What Tolkien calls the eucatastrophe—the good turn of events, the happy ending—is the most essential element in a fairy tale because it reflects the most essential truth of human existence: life has a happy ending; death isn't the end of the human story. Tolkien continues:

The consolation of fairy-stories, the joy of the happy ending: or more correctly of the good catastrophe, the sudden joyous "turn" (for there is no true end to any fairy-tale): this joy, which is one of the things which fairy-stories can produce supremely well, is not essentially "escapist," not "fugitive." In its fairy-tale—or otherworld—setting, it is a sudden and miraculous grace: never to be counted on to recur. It does not deny the existence of *dyscatastrophe,* of sorrow and failure: the possibility of these is necessary to the joy of deliverance; it denies universal final defeat and in so far is *evangelium,* giving a fleeting glimpse of Joy, Joy beyond the walls of the world, poignant as grief.[7]

For Tolkien, the eucatastrophic "sudden and miraculous grace" echoes in fantasy the same truth proclaimed in reality—in the good news of Jesus Christ *(evangelium)*: the everlasting joy of heaven is ours if we choose him who can lead us to it.

When Gaston discovers that the beast is real and that he stands in the way of his own desires, he rallies the townspeople to hunt down the beast and kill him. It leads to a final rooftop confrontation between the hunter and his beast of prey. "Did you honestly think she'd have you when she could have someone like me?" he shouts. "Belle is mine!" Inspired by seeing Belle return to the castle, the beast grabs Gaston by the neck and dangles him over the precipice. Looking into Gaston's now fearful eyes, the beast's own eyes change to express mercy to the hunter who would show no mercy to him, and he spares his life. As the beast moves toward his beloved Belle, Gaston, with skulls visible in the pupils of his eyes, mortally stabs the beast, and then falls to his own death.

With the orchestral love theme setting the scene, with rain falling around them, the beast says his good-bye: "You're back. At least I got to see you one last time," and he breathes his last. "Please, please don't leave me. I love you!" Belle declares as the last petal falls from the enchanted rose. Her declaration of love, given in her moment of greatest sorrow, makes possible great joy.

"Set me as a seal upon your heart...for love is strong as death," the Song of Songs declares" (8:6a, c). In truth, love is even stronger, as Christ showed us. Love breaks not only the enchanted spell of the beast, but also the heaviest of enchantments laid upon all of us beasts—death itself. In one of the best moments of eucatastrophe ever animated, the drops of rain begin to change into magical torrents of color, and as Alan Menken's musical score rises to a climax, the beast begins to transform. In order to prepare for drawing this scene, head animator of the beast, Glen Keane, studied Auguste Rodin's sculpture of *The Burghers of Calais* and Michelangelo's sculptures of slaves being freed from their bonds, to inspire his drawings of paws transforming into hands, hooves into feet, fur into skin—as the beast moves from animal to prince. This is the transformative moment, revealing on the outside who the beast is now on the inside, his moment of resurrection. While Keane and his team worked on the sketches, he kept posted on his storyboard a quote from Saint Paul to inspire him: "So if anyone is in Christ, there is a new creation: everything old has passed away; see, everything has become new!" (2 Cor 5:17).

After the beast is transformed, human once more, a new creation, he turns to his beloved Belle, who for a moment doesn't recognize him, until she looks into his eyes, the windows to the soul, and sees that he is truly the tortured soul—tortured no more—that she loves. Even then, with a handsome prince before her, Belle still looks beneath the surface.

Love never affects only the lover and beloved, for just as a rock thrown in a placid pond causes a ripple effect, the power of love that brings Beauty and the beast-no-more together transforms every molecule of the castle, making all things in the castle new again and all the characters human again, with the dark rain of death replaced by the color and light of rebirth—a scene that can stir the imagination to wonder about the end of days, when the glorified Christ resurrects all of humanity, and a new earth arises. Beauty and the beast live happily ever after for as long as they love one another.

It took two to break the spell. But the greater yoke had been placed on Belle, who was not subject to the spell, yet shouldered her burden better than Atlas. Blessed is Belle for not seeing, yet still believing. Belle found beauty in a beast, as have many other people over the years.

Beauty and the Beast debuted on November 13, 1991, to public and critical acclaim. It won a Golden Globe Award for Best Musical Comedy, and it was the first animated movie ever to be nominated for a Best Picture Academy Award. The accolades were so great that the film helped to validate animation as a legitimate art form. Walt Disney would have been proud. It has since been translated into a successful Broadway musical. Sadly, Howard Ashman, the film's executive producer and lyricist, who was mostly responsible for giving the film its vision and voice, died of AIDS a few months before the premiere date. The film credits carry a dedication to him: "To Howard: who gave a mermaid her voice and a beast his soul."

But the longer-lasting impact of *Beauty and the Beast* will be the timeless truths it conveys: beauty is found within, love triumphs, life has a happy ending, believing is seeing. These truths are, as Mrs. Potts sings, as certain as the sun that rises in the east; such is the tale of Beauty and the beast.

9

Jurassic Park

SCIENCE WITHOUT MORALS
IS MONSTROUS.

Amblin Entertainment / Universal Pictures (1993)

Producers	Kathleen Kennedy/Gerald R. Molen
Director	Steven Spielberg
Authors of Screenplay	Michael Crichton/David Koepp
Running Time	127 minutes

MAIN CHARACTERS

Dr. Alan Grant	Sam Neill
Dr. Ellie Sattler	Laura Dern
Dr. Ian Malcolm	Jeff Goldblum
John Hammond	Richard Attenborough
Tim Murphy	Joseph Mazzello
Lex Murphy	Ariana Richards

In the nineteenth century, European philosopher Ludwig Feuerbach optimistically proclaimed what he thought was the dawning of the Age of Man. Humankind, he believed, had grown up. We no longer needed infantile phantoms like God, who was merely the projection of our own greatness. Science, not religion, would take us to the next level in the evolution of consciousness, to the new paradise. In effect, science would become the new religion of the twentieth century. To summarize his philosophy in a simple formula: *Humanity invents god. Humanity destroys god. Humanity becomes god.* Feuerbach's philosophy, though supported by influential secular thinkers like Freud, Marx, and Nietzsche, was not without its critics. But slowly, over the course of the twentieth century, ideas like Feuerbach's began to trickle down and influence western culture. What the intelligentsia battled in ivory towers in the nineteenth century has today become the battles of the common people in the twenty-first century. And to the extent that science has been allowed to run without moral and religious restraint, we have seen modern culture look less like a Garden of Eden and more like a *Jurassic Park.*

In 1993, director Steven Spielberg delivered an action-adventure thriller set in a theme park unlike any that had ever been imagined by Disney. Based on a best-selling novel by Michael Crichton, *Jurassic Park* is the story of a scientific dream that becomes a nightmare. John Hammond, a brilliant and industrious scientist, by means of a scientific DNA breakthrough, genetically generates cloned dinosaurs after a sixty-five-million-year absence, on a remote island off the coast of South America. Confident in human ability to control and harness nature without consequences, Hammond creates a theme park for tourists. Before it opens, his investors insist on getting some outside opinions of the park's feasibility. Hammond recruits two dinosaur experts, paleontologist Dr. Alan Grant and paleobotanist Dr. Ellie Sattler, to spend a weekend at the island. Like Captain Nemo showing off the *Nautilus,* he is anxious for their approval. The team is joined by the wisecracking and skeptical Dr. Ian Malcolm, a mathematician who specializes in chaos theory, which involves determining variables and assigning probabilities to future events. Hammond's two grandchildren, Tim and Lex, join the three scientists. They are the first guests to preview the coming attraction. They have no idea of the adventure, "sixty-five million years in the making," that awaits them.

John Hammond is not an evil genius, but a genius who makes an evil decision. He is so intent on showing something special that he takes little account of its danger to the world. He is not a mad scientist bent on destruction; he is a reckless scientist bent on creation. He is so giddy with the greatness of his accomplishment that he doesn't think through the human implications. Even when events turn deadly, he still tries to minimize the danger. He casually explains, "All major theme parks have delays. When they opened Disneyland in 1956, nothing worked." To which, Ian Malcolm replies, "Yeah, but John, if the Pirates of the Caribbean ride breaks down, the pirates don't eat the tourists." Achieving a powerful scientific breakthrough was more dazzling to Hammond's ego than considering whether or not science had the capacity to control that power.

Anxious to impress them, Hammond tells the experts nothing prior to their visit. After dedicating years of their lives digging at archaeological sites, getting excited by fossil remains, Drs. Grant and Sattler are particularly awestruck by the sight of a majestic brachiosaurus and fascinated by the predatory power of a tyrannosaurus rex. Jurassic Park is an amazing accomplishment.

But to Hammond's surprise, all three experts are not overwhelmed with the prospects of an adventure park. Unlike him, they take a moment to consider the human cost that might be involved in such an endeavor. As impressive as Jurassic Park is, Dr. Malcolm is against it, in principle, from the start. "Don't you see the danger, John, inherent in what you're doing here? Genetic power is the most awesome of powers and you wield it like a kid who's just found his Dad's gun. I'll tell you the problem with the scientific power that you're using here: it didn't require any discipline to attain it." Malcolm accepts that there are consequences to messing with the natural order of things, to which Hammond's hubris has made him blind. Drs. Grant and Sattler are equally concerned, questioning how Hammond can assume control of an extinct ecosystem he knows virtually nothing about. As Alan explains, "Dinosaurs and man, two species separated by sixty-five million years of evolution, have just been suddenly thrown back into the mix together. How can we possibly have the slightest idea what to expect?" What the team couldn't have expected is how quickly the experience goes from awesome to awful.

Hammond had made some considerations for safety. A steel-cabled electrified fence encloses the dinosaurs, with the entire complex controlled by an advanced computer system. But there are two variables that Hammond never fully accounts for: Mother Nature and human nature. With a tropical storm brewing on the horizon, Hammond's unethical systems designer, Dennis Nedry, shuts down the park's computer system that had held the wild beasts at bay. In a short time, Hammond's carefully laid plans go awry. With the ecological environment no longer carefully contained, the dinosaurs' predatory aggressiveness takes over. The beasts break free to roam. Chaos has entered Hammond's ordered world. The natural instincts of the dinosaurs, sharpened by millions of years of natural selection, turn out to be more formidable than the naive but arrogant doctor ever anticipated. Before long the band of experts, along with Hammond's two grandchildren, are caught in the middle of the park, battling for their lives against the likes of vicious velociraptors and tyrannosaurus rex.

Much of *Jurassic Park*'s story line involves the team's fight for survival. It is, after all, a monster movie. After the T-Rex turns Hammond's lawyer, Donald Gennaro, into a late-afternoon snack, it terrorizes the two children trapped in a jeep. Dr. Grant comes to their aid as their jeep is pushed off a cliff. Able to assist the children in reaching safety down a tree, he must bring the kids through the park and outside the protective fencing. Back at the main control, Malcolm, Sattler, and Hammond work on restoring power while battling ferocious raptors.

After the dinosaurs threaten the children, Dr. Sattler realizes that scientific curiosity had gotten the better of her. She tells John, "I was overwhelmed by the power of this place, but I made a mistake, too. I didn't have enough respect for that power and it's out now. The only thing that matters now are the people we love: Alan, Lex, and Tim. John, they're out there where people are dying." The "people we love" ought to have been the *first* thing that mattered to Hammond, not the only thing left to be concerned about after it is too late.

Although *Jurassic Park* is best known for the film version's heart-stopping action adventure and big-budget special effects, the story is essentially a classic morality play. It serves as a warning against the current prevalent mentality of "science for the sake of science." The movie is not antiscience; in fact, the three invited visitors are all scientists by trade and rightfully proud of their vocation. Instead, like Mary Shelley's *Frankenstein, Jurassic Park* is a cautionary tale of the consequences of science without moral restraint. Even if humankind ignores the moral law, moral law will not ignore humanity. We will eventually destroy ourselves. If we set up scientific progress as an absolute, as Feuerbach proposed, humanity's regress will become the only certain absolute.

How did science, which has benefited our lives so much, become such a part of modern-day problems? To begin with, we trusted that science could do more than it should do. Science preserves its integrity only when it recognizes its natural limitations. Science cannot answer questions beyond what it was designed to answer by its own methodology.

On its own, science, simply does not have the answers to moral questions. It is not designed to that end. The hallmark of western civilization has been, in the words of Francis Bacon, "humanity's conquest of nature"—with one notable exception. We have not mastered human nature. Science has split the atom, but we also have split marriages. We have engineered DNA, but we have also engineered war. We have cured many diseases, but we have not cured loneliness. We have sent rockets to the heavens, but we have pushed heaven away from earth. We have improved the Internet, but not improved human interaction. We have mastered the computer, but not ourselves. Things may change, but human nature remains the same. Cultural and technological change cannot delude us into thinking that human beings have changed essentially. We find ourselves in the exact same position we have always been in: self-control still eludes us. Our problem is essentially a spiritual one.

"The complete lack of humility for nature that's being displayed here is staggering," comments Ian Malcolm. He is right. But logically, humility ought to extend not only to nature, but also to the Source behind nature's design—the Creator himself. If our will is not in tune with God's will, then science will not be the only disordered human endeavor. Eliminate God and we eliminate the one force in the universe that can subject all human beings, weak or powerful, to a common rule. Lacking ethical standards, the powerful will impose their desires on the weak—which is the definition of tyranny.

In *Jurassic Park*, tyranny may come in the form of a tyrannosaurus rex, but its rampage is the result of Hammond's hubris and Dennis Nedry's greed. In order to smuggle off the island dinosaur embryos that he will offer to the highest bidder, Nedry shamelessly risks the lives of innocents for profit. But like Kino's greed in Steinbeck's *The Pearl*, Nedry's greed for dinosaur embryos leads to his own demise, compliments of an acid-spewing dilophosaurus. Nedry is destroyed by the very wild nature from which he wished to profit.

Like Nedry, instead of shaping our behavior to conform to the truth, we can misuse technology and bend the truth to suit our behavior. In his book *The Abolition of Man*, C. S. Lewis identified perfectly this shift in thinking that exemplifies the modern, muddled mentality:

> For the wise men of old, the cardinal problem of human life was how to conform the soul to objective reality, and the solution was wisdom, self-discipline, and virtue. For the modern, the cardinal problem is how to conform reality to the wishes of man, and the solution is a technique.[8]

We have reached a point of tragic irony in the world of science. What was once scientific research for the benefit of humanity is now human research for the benefit of science. Instead of science profiting humankind, science now profits *from* humankind. Henry David Thoreau suggested this human tragedy when he wrote, "Men have become the tools of their tools."

Upon seeing *Jurassic Park* for the first time, my parenting instincts were tweaked right from the beginning. I recall being surprised that John Hammond would even *think* of bringing his two precious grandchildren to a remote island full of dinosaurs. Yet, in one sense, it is actually fitting that Hammond's own grandchildren are put in harm's way by his hubris. Children are often the first casualties of the expropriation of scientific power without regard to moral limits. With the abortion pill, we claim the power and the right to destroy innocent human embryos. With in vitro fertilization, we claim the power to freeze human embryos and discard them. With embryonic stem cell research, we claim the power to harvest human embryos like a crop. With cloning, we seek to kill one unique embryonic life and replace it with a different DNA-coded life of our choosing. Science has served the cause of slavery for the smallest, weakest, and most innocent of human beings.

Other examples of the misuse of science include the development of euthanasia drugs, suicide-assisting machines, health-endangering artificial contraception, performance-enhancing drugs, and chemical and biological weaponry. In a 1948 Armistice Day address, General Omar N. Bradley observed:

> We have too many men of science, too few men of God. We have grasped the mystery of the atom and rejected the Sermon on the Mount. The world has achieved brilliance without wisdom, power without conscience. Ours is a world of nuclear giants and ethical infants. We know more about war than we know about peace, more about killing than we know about living.

It is astounding that the same scientific community that is responsible for such horror has also given us great wonders such as antibiotics, vaccinations, open-heart surgery, cancer treatments, computers, cellular phones, air conditioning, airplanes, food preservation, and nutritional information. One would have to be ignorant not to recognize the benefits of scientific advancement that affect our daily lives. Truly, science can be part of the handiwork of God.

In 1999, the science fiction of *Jurassic Park* became scientific fact when geneticists reached a milestone in genetic engineering with the cloning of a sheep. They gleefully proclaimed to the news media "behold the lamb" as a sign of future things to come. But if cloning human beings ever becomes normative, then this lamb will become the new metaphor for the modern world. It will replace the "Lamb of God," who heralded the uniqueness of every individual and the ideal of procreating life in marital love, not in a test tube. Children could now be viewed solely as the genetic image of a human being, rather than as the image and likeness of God. Again, as Ian Malcolm accurately observes in *Jurassic Park,* referring to the choice to clone the dinosaurs, "Your scientists were so preoccupied with whether or not they could, they didn't stop to think if they should."

How has it been possible for science to become so out of moral focus? Some scientists, like so many in today's world, have fallen prey to the temptation inherent in power. When the soul is misdirected toward the acquisition of power, no material amount of power can ever satisfy it. Material medicine, in the form of power, cannot remedy a spiritual disease. No matter how much power we seek to acquire, we cannot find inner peace. It is like acquiring a million circles in pursuit of a square. The ability to control physical circumstances will never bring us an attitude of inner spiritual peace. The treasure of nobility, virtue, and human happiness lies where it always has—beyond the scope of the telescope, beyond the computations of computers. Only God can ultimately satisfy our needs. Science, in order to serve rather than be served, must discover what the comic book scientist Peter Parker discovered when he became the amazing Spider-Man: "With great power comes great responsibility." We need not *defy* science, just not *deify* it.

Set within suspenseful scenes of *Jurassic Park,* such as two hungry dinosaurs stalking Tim and Lex in the park's kitchen, we are given an example of the responsible scientist in the character of Dr. Alan Grant. While Grant marvels at the scientific spectacle of dinosaurs around him, he never loses his focus on the safety of the children. Although at first seemingly uncomfortable in his fatherly role, Alan discovers his own parental instinct in the process while guiding the children amid dinosaur danger.

When the moral law is ignored and evil is allowed to triumph disguised in the noble trappings of scientific pursuit, it is humankind that is ultimately victimized. Ever the mathematician, Ian Malcolm calculates a formula for the chaos of Jurassic Park. "God creates dinosaurs. God destroys dinosaurs. God creates man. Man destroys God. Man creates dinosaurs...." Dr. Ellie interjects the conclusion: "Dinosaurs eat man. Woman inherits the earth." Perhaps an even simpler formula, which reflects the danger inherent in Hammond and Feuerbach's philosophy, would be: *God creates humanity. Humanity rejects God. Humanity destroys humanity.* To the extent that the *Jurassic Park* warning is not heeded, humanity's story may not share the same happy ending that the film offers.

We have become the dinosaurs. If science advances without wisdom, humans will become an endangered species. We will suffer the same fate. The choice for humanity remains what it always has been and will be: either to choose the love of power or the power of love.

10

Rudy

GRACE BUILDS ON NATURE.
TriStar Pictures (1993)

Producer	Robert N. Fried
Director	David Anspaugh
Author of Screenplay	Angelo Pizzo
Running Time	116 minutes

MAIN CHARACTERS

Rudy Ruettiger	Sean Astin
Fortune	Charles S. Dutton
Daniel Ruettiger	Ned Beatty
Frank	Scott Benjaminson
Pete	Christopher Reed
Father Cavanaugh	Robert Prosky

A young aspiring actor was given this review by a Hollywood talent scout: "Can't act. Can't sing. Can dance a little." His name was Fred Astaire. She was a deaf, dumb, and blind girl whom many medical experts thought to be mentally retarded. Her name was Helen Keller. He was cut from his high school basketball team. His name was Michael Jordan. He was the all-time strike-out leader in baseball. His name was Babe Ruth. Tall, ugly, and uneducated, he lost virtually every political election he ever attempted. His name was Abraham Lincoln. He lived with racial prejudice as a young black man and faced derision targeted at him by the Nazi propaganda of Aryan supremacy at the 1938 Olympics. His name was Jesse Owens. Each of these people overcame adversity to display a greatness that was already within.

Each according to our gifts, each according to our choices, we hope to add our story to the list of stories that move from adversity to success, from sorrow to glory, from cross to crown. Or saying it another way, deep down inside we all want to be Rudy.

Rudy is the inspirational, slightly fictionalized story of Daniel "Rudy" Ruettiger, who, as an eleven-year-old boy, announced to his family, "After high school, I'm going to play football at Notre Dame." Lacking the size, the money, the athletic ability, and the grades for his dream to be possible, Rudy is told by his parents and teachers alike to give up his dream and set his sights a bit lower.

After playing his last high school football game for the Joliet Catholic "Hilltoppers," Rudy begins to realize that his dream of Notre Dame is more of an imposing mountaintop than a "hill." He is a dyslexic, below-average student who aspires to attend one of the top universities in the United States. He is a diminutive, average athlete who wants to play division-one football at one of the most competitive programs in the country. And so, Rudy gets a job in the steel mills, with Notre Dame slowly becoming "what might have been," until his friend Pete, the only person who believed that Rudy could make his dream a reality, dies tragically in an accident. The event propels Rudy into a decision that changes the course of his life. Donning the old Notre Dame jacket given to him as a gift by Pete, Rudy takes on his dream.

When it comes to personal dreams, *Rudy* is not about having it all. It is about having one dream to call your own. Rudy has to have the courage to lose one dream, marriage to Shelley, in order to aim at another, Notre Dame.

Rudy is not an epic story of grandeur. He doesn't lead troops in a historic battle or take the first step on the moon. Rudy is just an average guy, but it is the common people who have built the skyscrapers and plowed the fields of the world. Average soldiers, not generals, win a war. *Rudy* gives us a glimpse of how extraordinary the ordinary person really is.

Rudy is not a selfish story; it is a story about self-love. It's OK to pursue our dreams, to want heaven, to love ourselves. In fact, we are commanded to do so. Jesus' command to "love your neighbor as yourself" presupposes that we love ourselves. In our pursuit of meaningful dreams, we can find happiness, and happiness is infectious.

Rudy's dogged pursuit of his dream is inspiring. But what is most inspiring about the film lies in the manner of how those dreams come true.

Thomas Edison said that success is "10 percent inspiration and 90 percent perspiration." But in the story of *Rudy*, his 90 percent perspiration *is* inspiration for us. Rudy has "heart," which means he is willing to let it be broken. His father had advised him, "Chasing stupid dreams causes nothing but heartache." But herein lies the greatness of Rudy: he is willing to risk disappointment and pain. Heartache is the price paid for dreams purchased. Rudy's resolve is as hard as the steel milled in his blue-collar hometown.

With everyone predicting failure, especially his brother, Frank, Rudy chooses to try. Frank is envious of Rudy's aspiration for greatness. He lacks the courage to fail. He is afraid of the pain of disappointment. While Rudy's father is afraid for Rudy, Frank is afraid for himself. Sometimes the only failure is failing to try. Rudy's pursuit of his dream is not an act of rebellion. He does not hate his family or blame them for his problems. That would be wasted energy. Instead, he directs his energy toward his dream. Rudy seeks admission to Notre Dame not to spite his brother, but does so despite his brother.

With each passing semester of junior college, Rudy's admission to Notre Dame is rejected, but he continues to study for hours, keeps to his exercise regime, and works to pay the tuition bills. Like Rudy, we are all going to be knocked down in our lives. What we can control is whether we are going to get back up. No one is a loser who refuses the label. As Martin Luther King, Jr., said, "A man can't ride your back if you're standing up straight." Eleanor Roosevelt said, "No one can make you feel inferior without your consent." Suffering and disappointment, endured rightly, will not defeat us but increase us. Rudy's detractors underestimated him because they only measured in Rudy what they could see. But there is more to the human person than is shown in a mirror. Mirrors cannot measure the heart.

Perseverance, hope, sacrifice—these are Rudy's *be*-attitudes, his attitudes of being. Rudy takes responsibility for the one thing he can control in life, his attitude. There is always someone taller, stronger, faster, or brighter, but everyone has an equal chance to choose an attitude, to make his or her own heaven or hell.

"Have I done all that I can?" Rudy asks Father Cavanaugh, after receiving another rejection. Not even close. He hasn't done the most important thing. True success is a two-ingredient recipe: *ora et labora*—prayer and work. Prayer should not be a last resort, but the first. After trying everything, Rudy asks for guidance from the Savior who means everything. Saint Ignatius said, "Work as if everything depends on you, but pray as if everything depends on God." Ask and we shall receive. Rudy has the courage to ask God to help him become something more. In God's own way, he will receive. As Father Cavanaugh explains, "Answers come in God's time."

When we pursue a dream, we have to allow for unforeseen forks in the road. Rudy's is no different. His dream has to be adjusted to reality. Rudy had to wait five long years, just to begin his quest at age twenty-two. And even then, he is not able to attend Notre Dame for all four years, or necessarily be a starter on the football team, as he would have wished. Father Cavanaugh, Rudy's mentor since coming to Notre Dame, reminded Rudy that he has limits: "Son, in thirty-five years of religious study, I have only come up with two hard incontrovertible facts: there is a God, and I'm not him."

After many disappointments, Rudy finally reaches the first summit on his dream mountain. For his junior year, he is finally admitted into the University of Notre Dame. Having overcome so many obstacles, most people would have settled for that extraordinary accomplishment. But then again, most people aren't Rudy.

Having made it to the Notre Dame dormitory and classrooms, Rudy sets his sights a little higher. He wants to play football for the Fighting Irish.

Rudy is a David among gridiron Goliaths, armed with neither sling nor stone. He simply lacks the size and talent of the other players. But, amazingly, his determination and zeal win him a spot on the scout team. By simulating the next week's opposing team, the scout team specializes in being tackling dummies for the varsity. It's brutal work with little reward. Only a player that dresses for a varsity game is considered an official member of the team. Rudy and the scout team practice, but never play. Rudy's football dream falls short of being fulfilled.

Rudy's heart may have been in the right place, but his head wasn't always. The preamble to the Serenity Prayer reads, "God, grant me *serenity* to accept the things I cannot change, *courage* to change the things that I can, and *wisdom* to know the difference." Rudy exemplified courage, but he sometimes lacked serenity and wisdom.

"If it doesn't produce results, it doesn't mean anything. It's all been a waste," Rudy announces in frustration after he is first turned down for admission to Notre Dame. But his vision quest *had* produced results, just not the ones that Rudy wanted. Rudy couldn't see the intangible results of his pursuit of dreams. His maintenance boss, aptly named Fortune, provides a wake-up call: "You got your head so far up your ass about that damn football team; you don't get the fact that you just got a year of top quality education! Waste? Quit wasting my time!"

Still, Rudy continues to try to prove to everyone who doubted him that he "is somebody." But he *is* somebody whether he wins or loses. Rudy doesn't need to play a down of varsity football to earn his father's love or his brother's respect. Those are gifts freely given. They can't be coerced.

Similarly, we shouldn't pursue dreams to convince others of a worth we already possess. Intrinsic worth is not a prize we can achieve. It is a gift we have already been given. If we don't believe we have it, we never will, regardless of how many accomplishments we can list. We develop our gifts out of gratitude, not out of desperation. We pursue them to better ourselves, to become more than what we are. The hardships we face in pursuit of our dreams mold a stronger moral character, and therefore a greater capacity inside ourselves for happiness. If they do not, then we should either alter our attitude or stop pursuing dreams that are self-destructive.

When his last chance to dress for a varsity game in his senior year is seemingly gone, Rudy finally quits. He walks out before his last practice. Fortunately for him, there are guardian angels at Notre Dame. With strong words, Fortune again offers him an attitude adjustment:

> You're 5 foot nothin,' 100 and nothin,' and you have nearly a speck of athletic ability. And you hung in there with the best college football team in the land for two years. And you're getting a degree from the University of Notre Dame. In this life, you don't have to prove nothin' to nobody but yourself.

Rudy comes to realize what his teammates and friends have already realized—he *is* a success. True victory is more a matter of choice than chance. Rudy needed to realize that he had already benefited from his experience, even if he never played an official down. The journey was its own reward. When Rudy returns to his last practice, he does so resigned to the fact that he is never going to dress for a varsity football game. Playing in the final seconds of his final game would be icing on a cake that was already sweet.

If Rudy had not returned to his last football practice, he would not have received his moment in the sun. It would have been eclipsed by his own shadow.

The final triumphant scenes of *Rudy* are not a testimony to his abilities. His moment of personal glory is a moment of grace. The typical sports story ends with a championship game-winning feat by the hero—Roy Hobbs hits the winning home run in *The Natural* or Jimmy Chitwood shoots the game-winning shot in *Hoosiers*. But Rudy doesn't score the winning touchdown. His victory is a personal one, the fulfillment of a dream. Rudy does not bring victory to his team; his team brings victory to him.

In the end, Rudy alone does not achieve his dream of playing Notre Dame football. Rudy had climbed the mountain of his dreams as high as he could go. The dream is granted to him. One by one, the star players of the team lay down their jerseys, putting their varsity careers in jeopardy, offering up their spot on the team for Rudy. He is fortunate to be playing with teammates who judge a person not by his medals, but by his scars.

Rudy exemplifies the creed that *grace builds on nature.* His good fortune is another name for grace; grace is another name for God's blessings. As we strive for what is good, we open ourselves up to receive more grace. Fairy tales often illustrate the mystery of grace. It was Cinderella's compassion toward a beggar woman that led her to receive a magical gift from her fairy godmother. It is Rudy's perseverance and heart that lead to his moment of glory. Cinderella gets a gown and dances at the ball. Rudy gets a down and is carried off the field. Both go from rags to riches, from pauper to "prince" for a moment. The humble are exalted. Good works reveal real faith, and real faith receives moments of grace.

Rudy's moment of triumph is ultimately made possible by others. The unsung heroes of *Rudy* reach down and lift Rudy up. Carrying a player off the field is more a testament to the teammates who do the carrying, because at their moment of triumph, they are thinking of someone else more than themselves.

One lesson of *Rudy* is not simply that "nice guys finish first," it is that good guys always finish first. If not now, then later, but it will happen.

There is a danger of reducing the story to a speech on personal empowerment or a motivational blueprint for success: have a dream, set a goal, find a mentor, work the plan, never quit, and achieve the dream—case closed. But *Rudy* is not a testament to the power of positive thinking; rather, it reflects a "new testament" message that is timeless.

We have nothing to prove. We don't have to earn our worth. God loves us; it's all bonus. As my colleague and friend James Skerl once wrote, "God doesn't love us because we are good; God loves us because he is good." We don't have to earn heaven; it is a gift given freely. The phrase "unmerited grace," like the phrase "committed love," is similarly redundant, but necessary in a world that confusingly thinks that grace is earned and love can be free of responsibility. Like Rudy, our deepest dream of heaven cannot be reached alone. In the incarnation and resurrection, God reached down to lift us up to paradise. In Christ, God has carried a cross for us that we could not carry ourselves. To pursue heaven, we need only to have the courage to leave hell behind. That's the cross that comes before the crown.

Rudy is not just a story about Notre Dame, and yet in one important way, it is all about the vision that made Notre Dame. Just as Rudy endures and reaches his moment of triumph, there was once a humble girl who said *yes* to her destiny, who suffered and endured emotional swords that pierced her heart, and who, according to tradition, held her son's tortured, lifeless body in her arms. Yet, in the end, she became a queen; she became *Notre Dame,* "Our Lady," the sorrowful mysteries of her life turned glorious.

Rudy's moment of grace and glory is a metaphor for a far greater blessing that God will bestow on us. Mary has shown us the way. We can truly delight in Rudy's golden moment of grace under the golden dome. Onward to victory.

11

Groundhog Day

HAPPINESS IS GOODNESS.
Columbia Pictures (1993)

Producer	Trevor Albert
Director	Harold Ramis
Authors of Screenplay	Danny Rubin/Harold Ramis
Running Time	101 minutes

MAIN CHARACTERS

Phil Connors	Bill Murray
Rita	Andie MacDowell
Larry	Chris Elliott

Groundhog Day comes every February 2. Because it is one of the lesser holidays, it has retained much of its innocence and simplicity. It is a festival of winter, shadows, and the hope for spring. The same can be said of a romantic comedy of the same name that premiered in 1993. *Groundhog Day* is the story of Phil Connors, played by Bill Murray, an arrogant TV weatherman from Pittsburgh, Pennsylvania. Along with his producer Rita, played by Andie MacDowell, and cameraman Larry, he is sent to Punxsutawney to cover the annual Groundhog festival.

What Phil's weather forecast could not foresee was that magic awaited him in the air of Punxsutawney—a magic that would allow the character of Phil Connors and with him, the audience, to consider a great theological and philosophical question: What does it mean to be human? Wherein lies happiness?

Theological significance in a romantic comedy? It may be as unlikely to find religious insight in a romantic comedy as it is for Phil Connors to find true happiness in Punxsutawney, Pennsylvania, but both are there, if we have eyes to see and ears to hear. Through the magic in the film we can see the exact same day approached from the point of view of different life philosophies, with only one leading to happiness.

Life Philosophy One: Elitism and Fame

Although played with the wisecracking wit of Bill Murray, Phil Connors is a self-centered prima donna—in other words, a jerk. "People like blood sausage. People are morons," he declares. Our view of ourselves tends to be our view of others. This is equally true of Phil Connors. He is a cynical, elitist snob, who only wants to "get" from life, not "give." His character is in sharp contrast to Rita, whom director Harold Ramis described as a "mythical princess, pure in soul and spirit, beautiful, kind, generous, forgiving and honest"—values that are lost on Phil, at least initially. When Phil first meets Rita, he comments, "She's fun, but not my kind of fun." He holds her in the same esteem as he does the people of Punxsutawney, "They're hicks, Rita."

Miserable people tend to have miserable days. Unable to manipulate the circumstances of life in Punxsutawney on his very first day, he is left to his own unlikable self. He is as callous to a homeless man as he is to Rita and Larry. Snowed in by a blizzard, Phil is forced to stay overnight in Punxsutawney. But that is just the beginning of his troubles. His rotten day is not over; it has just begun. Phil wakes the next morning to discover that it is still Groundhog Day, still February 2. He has the same day to live over and over and over again.

In the magical transformation, he is exiled from his normal life, yet in his normal life, he is exiled from his own humanity. It leads us to a question: is the magic that happens to Phil Connors a good thing or a bad thing? It all depends on Phil. Would he see the cup as half-empty or half-full? Applying the same logic to us, might God create circumstances in our lives that are initially painful but may potentially lead to growth and happiness? Might not our greatest curse be a blessing in disguise? It all depends on us.

Life Philosophy Two: Destruction and Anarchy

Phil responds to his magical predicament in much the same way as he does his regular life—from a self-centered point of view. When he begins to realize that there might be some personal advantages to having no tomorrow, and therefore no consequences to his actions, Phil lets his meanness out. He can be as nasty as he wants to be. He can get drunk and drive his car on the train tracks or punch the irritating life insurance salesman, Ned Ryerson. "I'm not going to live by their rules anymore," Phil declares.

Although Phil does not have to deal with the external consequences of his actions, he still has to deal with the emotional and spiritual consequences those actions have on him internally. As it turns out, his self-centered fantasies are not as fantastic as he had imagined them. The life of an egocentric god has moments of short-lived pleasure and conquest, but they leave him empty. The initial thrill of recklessness is fleeting and incomplete. Phil wants something more. He just doesn't know where to find it.

Life Philosophy Three: Hedonism

Knowledge is indeed power, but power alone does not lead to happiness. It can, however, lead to pleasure. Having knowledge of how the day progresses, Phil manipulates the circumstances of his day like no ordinary person can. He becomes wealthy, gorges himself on food, and manipulates a local girl, Nancy, for sex. Despite every selfish fantasy being met, he is still vacuous. He wants more. So do we.

Phil's days of wine, women, and hedonism keep repeating and repeating, long enough for him to realize what he really wants—Rita—the one woman of substance in his life. Phil hopes that her happiness will rub off on him. "What I really need is someone like you," he tells Rita. But like a tricycle-bound child who wants to get behind the wheel of a real race car, he can't handle the track of true love. Why not? The reason is simple: Phil does not love.

Phil tries everything to create the pretense of love for Rita. He recites French poetry to her, shares her favorite drink, pretends to value family and friends as she does, but it doesn't work. His campaign to win her over fails. Phil can't have Rita, because she is not a possession to be had. Try as he does, he cannot manipulate love out of her. Rita declares, "This whole day has been one long set up. I could never love someone like you because you'll never love anyone but yourself." Rita's right. Phil is incapable of receiving the love he desperately wants from Rita. He lacks the depth of character to attract a person of substance.

The one pleasure Phil wants to experience eludes him. He can't have it because love is not a pleasure; it is a joy. Pleasure is sweet; love is bittersweet. Like a spoiled child refusing his vegetables and grabbing for the candy, Phil avoids the bitter and only wants the sweet. In the process, he has become a bitter man.

Socrates said that "an unexamined life is not worth living," but in Phil Connors' case, an unlived life is not worth examining. Rita grasps this when she quotes to him a poem from Sir Walter Scott:

> The wretch, concentered all in self.
> Living shall forfeit fair renown,
>> and doubly dying, shall go down
>> to the vile dust from whence he sprung,
>> unwept, unhonored, and unsung.

The truth hurts as it heals. There is little left for Phil except to see the wretch he has become.

Life Philosophy Four: Despair and Nihilism

The forecast for Phil's future looks bleak: "It's going to be cold; it's going to be gray. And it's going to last you for the rest of your life." Unable to manipulate his circumstances to create any joy, Phil is left with himself. But he doesn't like himself. "I've come to the end of me, Rita. There's no way out," Phil confesses somberly. But there is one way out. What Phil hasn't realized yet is that at the end of "me" is the beginning of others. Thus, Phil blows himself up, gets hit by a speeding bus, and is stabbed, shot, frozen, burned, and electrocuted. But no matter what he does, he wakes up the next morning with the same day to live all over.

Phil learns that suicide is futile. No matter what Phil does, "he" remains. Here we have one of the most truthful representations of suicide in modern films. As Catholic writer Peter Kreeft noted, "Suicide doesn't work. You can't kill your soul, and that's where you feel the pain." Suicide solves nothing. It only exacerbates the misery.

Life Philosophy Five: Romantic Love (Eros)

Finally, Phil acts honestly. Having tried and failed to alter his predicament in the most radical of ways, he finally has a moment of grace. Instead of trying to change reality to suit himself, he tries to change himself to suit reality. He moves from self-centered to other-centered. The fifth life approach is genuine romantic love. He spends an honest day with Rita, no longer trying to manipulate her, no longer seeing her as an object for his pleasure but as a real person. And by seeing her for who she really is, he sees himself for who he really is. As he says to Rita, "It's all right, I am a jerk." Seeing her goodness reveals to him his own narcissism. Through Rita, he sees himself truly, and he learns what love is all about. He values her and not just her body. Instead of trying to touch her, he is "touched" by her. He experiences the bittersweet joy of loving another person, and learns to honor and cherish one woman completely. As she falls asleep next to him, Phil finally speaks from his heart:

I think you're the kindest, sweetest, prettiest person I have ever seen in my whole life. I've never seen anyone that's nicer to people than you are. The first time I saw you something happened to me. I never told you, but I knew that I wanted to hold you as hard as I could. I don't deserve someone like you, but if I ever could, I swear I would love you for the rest of my life.

Phil acknowledges genuine weakness and it is his first moment of strength. As Saint Paul wrote, "My grace is sufficient for you, for power is made perfect in weakness" (2 Cor 12:9).

At this point in the story, we are given a glimpse of the typical romantic-comedy happy ending. Romantic love has begun to save him, just as a good woman has helped save many a man (and vice versa) over the centuries. This is where Hollywood usually ends its stories, extolling the virtues of romantic love. But quite amazingly, this movie takes the next step and goes from what was a good story to a great one.

Life Philosophy Six:
Love Thy Neighbor (Agape)

Even after making the huge stride of loving one person, Phil still wakes up to the same song on the radio on the same February 2. Instead of stopping at valuing Rita, he must go further. If loving Rita showed him the truth about himself, why not love others as well? Maybe every person is as special as Rita, each in his own way? Perhaps the joy that Phil experienced in his genuine longing for Rita can be found elsewhere in different forms? Maybe true human growth comes from seeing the goodness that is present in others? Maybe if he divides his love, he multiplies his joy? His own personal suffering has made him empathetic to others. And so, Phil sets out to love his neighbor.

In doing so, Phil shatters the shallowness of all his previous life philosophies. He becomes present to the moment, rather than allowing ambition for future power and fame to blind him. He becomes creative, taking up music and ice sculpting, rather than seeking the fleeting pleasure and enduring pain of destruction. He chooses to self-sacrifice for others rather than to manipulate people for fleeting moments of sexual pleasure. Much to the dismay of the Playboy empire, there is more to this world than appetite. Phil finds meaning in his life, rather than turning to nihilism. He chooses to love in small ways, as in changing a flat tire or saving a child from a fall. In doing so, he moves from his eros-love of one person, Rita, to agape-love of many.

Groundhog Day presents the beautiful irony of romantic love. Phil ceases to make Rita the object of his life. Instead, he builds a life for himself in serving others, and he is served in the process. As the depth of his personhood increases, Rita can now be attracted to him. When he abandons his narrow quest for Rita, she finds him. The perfect day does not culminate in sex, as it does in most romantic comedies these days, but in love. When he gives up Rita as the focus of his life, he receives her love back. Phil lives out the paradox of love. He receives the prize of romantic love only after he prizes others.

Life Philosophy Seven: Love of God?

Groundhog Day is a wonderful story, but it has its limitations, as do all stories. It never explains the origin of the time warp in which Phil finds himself. It does not include a seventh step that would take philosophy to the higher level of religion, and move the viewer from love to recognition of faith. We never learn why the miracle is occurring for Phil Connors. We never find out who is behind it, even though God is the most likely candidate. Phil never takes the final step to recognize the God that dwells in each and every person of Punxsutawney, though he more importantly lives out this truth. He begins to recognize his neighbor both near and far, but his gaze never turns upward. Like many who love their neighbor as themselves, Phil never makes the connection that he is, in fact, loving God by loving them. Hollywood often avoids the "faith dimension" for fear that it might alienate its audience. The limitation of this "seventh seal" never being broken can also be, in one way, the film's strength. It makes the film accessible to any person whose religion, formal or otherwise, believes that happiness lies in loving one's neighbor.

Just as Phil never consciously recognizes God in his neighbor, most of us don't realize that worship of God lies within the tradition of Groundhog Day. The holiday was brought to America by German settlers in the 1700s, who celebrated the early Christian tradition of Candlemas Day—a festival of light set at the midpoint of winter, where people would have candles blessed and then placed in their windows, to remind themselves that the light of Christ remained even in the dark of winter. A tradition developed that if people would see their shadows on that day, there would be six more weeks of winter weather. As an old Scottish rhyme says, "If Candlemas Day is bright and clear, there'll be two winters in the year." Over time, an ancient belief that animals could sense the beginning of spring became wedded with the celebration. Eventually, the tradition centered on the hedgehog seeing its shadow. In America, it became the groundhog, with the oldest recorded tradition of the festival coming from none other than Punxsutawney, Pennsylvania.

In the process of loving, Phil learns that he cannot do everything. Try as he does, he cannot save the dying homeless man. Like all of us, he can only do some good, not all good. But we are not judged by the quantitative effect of our love, only by its quality. Mother Teresa simply stated, "To show great love for God and our neighbor we need not do great things. It is how much love we put in the doing that makes our offering something beautiful for God."

Phil accepts the weather conditions of his life and improves his extended outlook. He learns to accept the circumstances that he cannot control, and instead controls his attitude toward those circumstances. In doing this, Phil is no longer a prisoner of a time and place. He is free to enjoy a winter day and able to sculpt a life of love that will last long after the ice melts.

Phil Connors declares, "Winter, slumbering in the open air, wears on his smiling face a dream of spring." Every moment is pregnant with possibilities. The same day that had once brought him to total despair now provides an opportunity to love. Instead of seeking his own happiness first, Phil lets happiness find him. The happiness was always there, as is our God, patiently waiting for us to turn toward the divine light. Phil allows the audience to realize that happiness is intertwined with goodness. "No matter what happens tomorrow or for the rest of my life, I'm happy now, because I love you." Phil's happy ending is a new beginning as he finds happiness in love.

Now that Phil has transformed himself, Punxsutawney no longer seems so terrible. In a final irony, when the story ends, he talks of living there permanently. Hell has become heaven.

> When Chekhov saw the long winter, he saw a winter bleak and dark and bereft of hope. Yet we know that winter is just another step in the cycle of life. But standing here among the people of Punxsutawney and basking in the warmth of their hearths and hearts, I couldn't imagine a better fate than a long and lustrous winter.

Phil Connors is given a precious gift—the chance to get the day right. So are we. We are under the same weight of time that Phil endures. As routine as our days might seem—same bed, alarm clock, family, job, house, town—we, too, are given the chance to get it right, to God's satisfaction, and transform the way we "see" our circumstances.

In order for his day to stop repeating, Phil had to realize the fullest potential of love that is present in one Groundhog Day in Punxsutawney. His own selfishness had been blocking the light of happiness. He had to get out of his own way. In other words, Phil Connors' day stops repeating when he stops seeing his shadow.

12

The Shawshank Redemption

HOPE IS TRUE FREEDOM.

Castle Rock Entertainment / Columbia Pictures (1994)

Producer	Niki Marvin
Director	Frank Darabont
Author of Screenplay	Frank Darabont
Running Time	142 minutes

MAIN CHARACTERS

Andy Dufresne	Tim Robbins
Red Redding	Morgan Freeman
Warden Samuel Norton	Bob Gunton
Captain Byron Hadley	Clancy Brown
Tommy Williams	Gil Bellows
Brooks Hatlen	James Whitmore

Why do bad things happen to good people? This is a question that we have been wrestling with since Adam and Eve ate the forbidden fruit. But *The Shawshank Redemption* answers a more relevant question: when bad things happen to good people, what should good people do?

To say that bad things happen to the main character of *The Shawshank Redemption,* Andy Dufresne, is putting it mildly. Andy is sentenced to life imprisonment for a crime he did not commit. The circumstances pointed in a direction that was opposite the truth. Circumstances won the verdict. "I'll see you in hell before I see you in Reno," Andy had said to his wife the night of her murder. But it is Andy who is sent to a hell that goes by the name of Shawshank Prison.

American movie audiences have always had an interest in prison dramas. Successful actors, as well, have been drawn to them—Burt Lancaster in *Birdman of Alcatraz,* Steve McQueen in *Papillon,* Burt Reynolds in *The Longest Yard,* Paul Newman in *Cool Hand Luke,* Robert Redford in *Brubaker,* and Tom Hanks in *The Green Mile.* Why such an interest? Prison is a world that most of us will never know but rightfully fear. And therein lies its fascination.

Just as Dostoyevsky's *Crime and Punishment* made us admire the "noble prostitute," Hollywood's "innocent prisoner" holds a similar fascination. Practically speaking, in the real world, most of us are willing to concede that the vast majority of prisoners are in prison because they deserve to be, and the legal system, though flawed, generally tries to do its best, and prison wardens and guards do difficult, honest work. But turning this world upside down in fiction, placing an innocent prisoner into a corrupt legal system with evil, power-hungry prison officials, allows us to wonder, "What would it be like if I were unjustly sent to prison? What would I be like?"

The innocent prisoner in *The Shawshank Redemption,* which is based on a novella by Stephen King, is a former wealthy banker, cool and aloof in manner, and oddly intellectual. Andy Dufresne does not appear to be very inspiring. But appearances can be deceiving, and time has a way of whittling away at our deceptions, revealing the real person. Time is one thing that Andy has in abundance.

But time is not all that Andy has. He finds a treasured commodity, one that is precious inside or outside prison—a friend. Red Redding is the kind of prisoner who has inside connections to get another prisoner anything he desires; yet he is drawn to Andy because Andy has something he needs, something you can't buy or bargain for.

For the first two years, Andy's life consists of choosing his own nightmare, either brutal beating from the guards or brutal rape from sadistic inmates. Again, he appears the weak victim. But he is not.

The years of brutality do not make Andy brutal. His interior life gives him a sense of peace, which is mistaken for snobbishness. He survives prison the only way any of us can survive life: he immerses himself in what is meaningful to him. He lives out what Thomas More wrote: "The times are never so bad that a good man cannot live in them." Andy passes the hours in his cell by carving chess pieces of alabaster and soapstone, to play a civilized game of kings, with only a Rita Hayworth poster to keep him company.

The first window into Andy's strength of character comes when he bargains with the meanest guard in Shawshank, Byron Hadley, volunteering to set him up a tax-free savings account. Andy only asks for three beers for each of the work crew in exchange for his service. More than just finding an ally against the more savage inmates, Andy risks punishment for a moment of humanity under the sun. The gamble pays off. Red, who functions as both narrator and key character, describes the experience:

> We sat with the sun on our shoulders and drank like free men. Hell, we could have been tarring the roof of one of our own houses. We were the lords of all creation. As for Andy—I think he did it just to feel normal again, if only for a short while.

Assisting his fellow prisoner, Brooks Hatlen, in the library, Andy serves as financial advisor for all the guards. Then Brooks is paroled. After fifty years in prison, however, he has become used to the walls he once hated. Prison life is all he knows, and it has taken away his capacity to create a life for himself. Brooks is freed from Shawshank Prison, but he is not free. A halfway house bed and a job bagging groceries are not enough. Still a prisoner of his own mind, he finally tires of being afraid and uncertain on his own. Tragically, he kills himself.

Years go by, and Andy continues to hold on to hope. By chance, he is given another opportunity to feel human again. He takes it. Discovering an old Italian phonograph record, Andy broadcasts its music throughout the whole prison (similar to what the character Guido does in *Life Is Beautiful*) and locks the door and listens. The soul thirsts for beauty. Again, Red reflects on the moment:

I have no idea to this day what those two Italian ladies were singing about. Truth is, I don't want to know. Some things are best left unsaid. I like to think they were singing about something so beautiful it can't be expressed in words, and makes your heart ache because of it. I tell you those voices soared, higher and farther than anybody in a gray place dares to dream. It was like some beautiful bird flapped into our drab little cage and made those walls dissolve away. And for the briefest of moments, every man in Shawshank felt free.

Art can elevate our spirit, and remind us that we have one. After two weeks in solitary confinement, Andy emerges spiritually unscathed. However, he discovers that his attitude toward prison life is not the same as Red's.

"Easiest time I ever did. I had Mozart to keep me company in here [my head] and here [my heart]. That's the beauty of music. They can't get that from you. You need music so you don't forget."

"Forget what?"

"Forget that there are places in the world that aren't made of stone. That there is something inside that they can't get to, that they can't touch. It's yours."

"What are you talking about?"

"Hope."

"Let me tell you something my friend. Hope is a dangerous thing. Hope can drive a man insane. It's got no use on the inside. You'd better get used to that idea."

"Like Brooks did?"

Andy understands that it was Brooks's lack of hope that drove him to the insanity of suicide. Despair is dangerous; hope is the sanity of salvation.

While psychiatrist Victor Frankl was in the Nazi concentration camp in Auschwitz, he discovered that without a capacity for hope, prisoners would lose their spiritual strength and begin to decay psychologically and physically. Human survival depended on a faith in the future. In his insightful work *Man's Search for Meaning*, Frankl tells the story of a prisoner who had had a dream telling him that the prisoners would be liberated on March 30 of that year. Initially, the dream filled him with hope. Frankl then recounts what occurred:

> When F— told me about the dream, he was still full of hope and convinced that the voice of his dream would be right. But as the promised day drew nearer, the war news which reached our camp made it appear very unlikely that we would be free on the promised date. On March twenty-ninth, F— suddenly became ill and ran a high temperature. On March thirtieth, the day his prophecy had told him that the war and suffering would be over for him, he became delirious and lost consciousness. On March thirty-first, he was dead. To all outward appearance, he had died of typhus.[9]

But the inward significance is clear. The loss of hope had a deadly effect. And although the conditions in a prison camp are far more brutal than the ones faced by the average individual, the principle remains the same: hope is necessary for human survival. Pearl Buck once wrote, "To eat bread without hope is still slowly to starve to death." We all seek exile from the confines of human existence, which include suffering, illness, and death. As the prisoner in Frankl's story illustrates, hope is the life-blood of the human soul.

In the real concentration camp at Auschwitz and the fictional Shawshank Prison, the message is the same: hope is a vital part of the human condition. But what is the object of hope? Here, the angels of faith enter where Hollywood secularists fear to tread. Saint Thomas Aquinas pointed out that hope has a twofold object: "the eternal life we hoped for and the divine help we hope by." Hope, fully understood, is directed toward the one thing in the universe that cannot disappoint, that cannot fail us—God. The true object of hope, then, is a divine promise made: God loves us and he will not abandon us. It is assured by promises kept in the past. God has never broken a promise; he is true to his word. A person of hope leans on that promise through the nights and lives that promise through the days.

Andy's talent in assisting the guards with financial advice does not go unnoticed. Warden Norton uses Andy's abilities to set up phony accounting records to launder money that secretly fills his own pockets. Norton is a whitened sepulcher, white and polished on the outside, spouting biblical platitudes, but rotten and corrupt on the inside. Andy's fake accounts make him a valuable commodity for the warden. And that is how he is treated—as a commodity, not a human being.

Andy uses his position to build up the quality of the prison library and to educate cons toward earning their high school diplomas, particularly Tommy Williams, a young inmate eager to reform. And it turns out that Tommy can aid Andy, as well. Tommy had met a cellmate at another prison who admitted to him that he had killed Andy's wife. Andy now has a legitimate way out, at least a new trial. But Shawshank Prison is far from legitimate. The warden has Tom Williams permanently silenced to keep Andy a permanent resident. Andy is put in solitude for over a month.

Andy reaches his breaking point. A victim of circumstance, he was now a victim of corruption. The fragile peace that had sustained him for all those years now seemed in danger of cracking. "I guess it comes down to a simple choice, really. Get busy living, or get busy dying," he listlessly tells Red.

Red fears the worst. If a friend is the answer to our needs, then it was Andy's resiliency that had drawn Red's admiration. Now, Red worried. "I've had some long nights in stir. Alone in the dark with nothing but your thoughts, time can draw out like a blade. That was the longest night of my life."

Sometimes when the darkness lasts a long time, it makes the light seem that much brighter when it finally comes. As narrated so eloquently by Red,

> In 1966, Andy Dufresne escaped from Shawshank Prison....Andy crawled to freedom through five hundred yards of smelling foulness I can't even imagine. Maybe I just don't want to. Five hundred yards. That's the length of five football fields. Just shy of half a mile.

Andy emerges from the sewer pipe, tears off his shirt, smiles, and raises his gaze to the sky, feeling the rain on his face and back. The rains are the waters of baptism, marking the end of his prison drought. Andy can begin again. For him, Shawshank Prison was never a hell. He never let it become so. It was a purification where he atoned for any mistakes he may have made in his life. On that rainy night, Andy's purgatory led to his Shawshank redemption.

Andy's extraordinary escape matches his extraordinary nineteen-year ordeal. We can't help but rejoice along with him. But there is one missing piece. Can Andy's redemption extend to Red? Upon being granted parole after a forty-year sentence, Red is finally freed. But is he free?

Freedom that is understood as only external behavior denies the inner struggle to master ourselves. The choice to do what is right frees us from the tyranny of emotion dictated by circumstance. When we lose our inner freedom to will what is good, we also lose the self-respect that flows from being in control of our own lives. Saint Augustine grasped this paradox.

In an age when we can most change our material circumstances, we are most miserable. Money, fame, or power cannot make us happy. At best, they can only provide circumstances that are more conducive to happiness. But happiness ensues from a change in self, not from a change in the world. Happiness comes from an attitude of being, a "*be*-attitude," that is freely chosen within. This was the glorious message of the ultimate freedom fighter, Jesus Christ, who conquered all that had enslaved us, and then, with the exuberance of a child, shouted across the cosmic playground, "Ollie, Ollie, everybody's free! Come out of hiding." Christ has freed us from the grip of sin and offers us the grace to master our selfish impulses. Freedom is not a word first written on a parchment as a constitution, but a secret word written on human hearts since the beginning of time that shapes the human constitution. We are free. Circumstances might control our bodies, but they need not control our spirits. We hold the final card. We have the power to choose love in the midst of hate, truth in a world of lies, freedom in a world of slavery, God in a world of loneliness.

When the desperate make their prison break from God under the banner cry of "freedom," in that instant, unbeknown to them, they chain themselves to something or someone else. As George MacDonald wrote, "A man is in bondage to whatever he cannot part with that is less than himself." Freedom is too precious a gift to be traded for cheap grace. The truly human person has found freedom in the paradox of love. By serving God and abiding by religious and moral principles, we are free of anything or anyone that would enslave our soul. We find freedom only when we submit to the One who deserves our submission. The proper end of submission is God. In bending our knee, our humanity is raised up. Submit to the voice of conscience, and we become free of the tyranny of popular opinion. Submit to a path of goodness, and we become free from evil's darkness. In other words, submit to God, which is the essence of true religion, and taste freedom.

Will Red go the way of Andy or the way of Brooks Hatlen? Did the institution become a part of Red, or can he part from the institution? The outside world is a stranger, and he is forty years out of date. Fear makes Red contemplate going back inside where things make sense. But like Christ's resurrection, one man's redemption never affects him alone. His friend reaches out to Red via a letter and invites him to begin again. Under a tree in a summer meadow, Andy's letter ends with a message to Red and to us.

"Remember, Red, hope is a good thing. Maybe the best of things. And no good thing ever dies."

Love, in the form of friendship in Red's case, can destroy fear. With hope, there is the real freedom to dream meaningful dreams that fill a heart with joy and the courage to live. Red makes his choice to live again.

> Get busy living or get busy dying. That's damn right....I find I'm so excited I can barely sit still or hold a thought in my head. I think it's the excitement only a free man can feel, a free man at the start of a long journey whose conclusion is uncertain. I hope I can make it across the border. I hope to see my friend and shake his hand. I hope the ocean is as blue as it has been in my dreams. I hope.

Hope *is* the best of things. Hope is faith pointed toward the future. It energizes and revitalizes the present in anticipation of a future glory that is seen as possible. Andy's path to redemption from Shawshank Prison is our path to redemption from our prison—imprisoned in our own failures, bad habits, character flaws, life situations, age, family, health. As a consequence of original sin, we are all in a prison of our own making, affected by circumstances not always of our own choosing. Prison can be either a hell that breaks us or a purgatory that makes us. Life can be either a hopeless end or an endless hope. The choice is ours—heaven or hell—in this life, as well as the next. Get busy living or get busy dying.

13

Forrest Gump

LOVE IS AS LOVE DOES.

Paramount Pictures (1994)

Producer	Wendy Finerman
Director	Robert Zemeckis
Author of Screenplay	Eric Roth
Running Time	142 minutes

MAIN CHARACTERS

Forrest Gump	Tom Hanks
Jenny Curran	Robin Wright
Lieutenant Dan Taylor	Gary Sinise
Mrs. Gump	Sally Field

Imagine a film that is not exactly a comedy, yet it is not a pure drama. It is not a particularly happy story, but its mood is not all sadness. It is not necessarily an inspirational story; still, there is a message to its madness. Confused? Welcome to the wonderful world of *Forrest Gump*.

Watching a film like *Forrest Gump* is a little like being Alice through the looking glass. Things are a little strange. Even Forrest's name is odd. He is named after the great Confederate General Nathan Bedford Forrest, who goes on to found the Ku Klux Klan. His mother gives him the name to remind him that sometimes people do things that make no sense. Forrest will need that sense of humility. He has an IQ of seventy-five, five points below the cut-off of what is considered normal. He is mentally slow and, as a boy, has to wear braces on his legs to help correct the curvature of his spine. Abandoned by his father, he is raised solely by his mother, who dedicates herself to giving Forrest the best life she can.

Given his unfortunate circumstances, we might suspect that Forrest will inevitably become a tragic figure, a Willie Loman, pulled down by his mental deficiency and chained by the iron braces that surround his legs. But we would be wrong. In a scene that reveals his real destiny, young Forrest is being taunted and chased by cruel boys on bicycles. His friend, Jenny, is shouting, "Run, Forrest, run!" Struggling to get away, in slow motion, we see the metal braces break off, and Forrest runs like the wind. His back is healed, and he easily outdistances the bullies. This is the metaphor for Forrest's life. Amazingly, he will transcend the hate and hardship around him and run free.

In the standard formula of drama, the main character undergoes an event that changes him, that forces him to make a choice. He is either transformed by the event or scarred. Little Red Riding Hood must contend with a scheming wolf. Hamlet seeks justice for his father. King Midas is cursed by his own greed for gold. But like a photographic negative that inverts color, *Forrest Gump* is the exact opposite of a typical drama. He remains essentially the same, while all around him, the world changes for the good and, particularly, for the bad.

The tragedy in the film is not Forrest; it is the world around him. Forrest Gump is the calm in the eye of a tornado. The tornado is the turbulent individuals that surround his life and that reflect the greater turbulence in the American culture of the 1950s through the 1980s.

Jenny Curran is Forrest's childhood sweetheart. He calls her "my most special friend, my only friend." Like peas and carrots, they bond throughout their childhood years, spending time sitting on tree limbs, talking and laughing. Forrest describes her voice as "the voice of an angel." But she is a broken angel. Her life is opposite that of Forrest, who is outwardly slow and odd, but is loved by his Momma. Jenny, on the other hand, has the outward appearance of success: intelligence, good looks, and popularity, but on the inside she lives with the trauma of sexual abuse caused by her incestuous father. And even though her father died when Jenny was still young, the memories haunt her. When she reaches adulthood, she falls prey to the emerging 1960s counterculture, which initiates her into a pattern of personal excess and sexual abuse.

Jenny's life is a destructive search for love. She dates the wrong kind of guy, becomes sexually loose, experiments with drugs, and involves herself in abusive relationships. But regardless of her choices, Forrest is always there for Jenny. When he witnesses her making out in the back seat of a car with her date, he immediately runs over and punches the guy. Forrest instinctively knows that Jenny is doing something wrong, something that will hurt her. He may lack intelligence, but he does not lack wisdom.

Being sexually innocent, Forrest is a safe haven for Jenny. She cares about Forrest, but she doesn't value his innocence; instead, she overlooks it in her search for happiness. She wants something more from life; she wants to be famous. She longs for the validation of strangers. "Do you have a dream, Forrest, about who you're gonna be?" Jenny asks Forrest. Confused, he replies, "Who am I gonna be? Aren't I going to be me?" Fame doesn't matter to Forrest; he already has value. Her path to fame leads Jenny to performing at a strip bar. When a rowdy customer gropes at her, Forrest leaps to the stage and tries to rescue her. "I can't help it; I love you, Jenny," Forrest explains. Jenny responds, "Forrest, you don't know what love is." She couldn't be further from the truth.

More than any other scene, Jenny's musical debut at the strip bar provides the quintessential symbol of what was wrong with the counterculture: Jenny sits nude on the stage of a strip bar, with drunken men yelling for sexual stimulation, while she sings an acoustic rendition of Dylan's "Blowin' in the Wind." She sings a meaningful song in a meaningless place with men mindful only of her naked body—a scene deserving a nomination for the "Irony Hall of Fame." And they call Forrest Gump stupid.

Forrest's and Jenny's lives move in opposite directions. Forrest joins the Army and fights in Vietnam; Jenny joins the counterculture and fights the Army. Jenny drops acid while Forrest drinks Dr. Pepper. When Jenny's pseudointellectual boyfriend slaps her across the face, Forrest, again, instinctively tackles him and thrashes him. Forrest protects whom he loves. His intelligence might be limited, but his love, especially for Jenny, is unlimited. He doesn't deal intellectually with the issues of the day; he deals with the day. He doesn't wrestle with contemporary ideas; he wrestles people who might hurt Jenny. The love Jenny needed was so close to her, yet it took her a lifetime to notice it.

Forrest Gump is a man of peace in the midst of the two most controversial wars in recent American history: the Vietnam War, halfheartedly begun by the establishment, and the culture war, zealously begun by the counterculture, ironically, under the flag of freedom and peace. Forrest's commanding officer in Vietnam, Lieutenant Dan Taylor, becomes a casualty of the first, and his beloved Jenny becomes a victim of the second. Both Lieutenant Dan and Jenny were caught on the losing side.

Lieutenant Dan Taylor is a decent person and a good military leader. He comes from a line of Taylors who have fought and died in every single American war. When his platoon is caught in enemy fire, shrapnel hits his legs. Like his forefathers before him, he passively accepts that it is his time to die with honor on the battlefield. But Lieutenant Dan's understanding of destiny didn't account for Forrest Gump. Having initially escaped the conflict, Forrest runs back into harm's way, carrying wounded men on his back, including Lieutenant Dan. "Leave me here! I said, leave me here!" But Forrest ignores the order. He instinctively knows that life is sacred and should be saved. He demonstrates incredible bravery. Forrest saves his life, but the recuperating Lieutenant Dan is far from grateful:

> "Now, you listen to me. We all have a destiny. Nothing just happens. It's all part of a plan. I should have died out there with my men. But now, I'm nothing but a g--d--- cripple, a legless freak! Look. Look at me. Do you know what it's like not to be able to use your legs? Did you

hear what I said? You cheated me. I had a destiny. I was supposed to die in the field with honor. That was my destiny! And you cheated me out of it! Do you understand what I'm saying, Gump? This wasn't supposed to happen, not to me. I had a destiny. I was Lieutenant Dan Taylor."

"You're still Lieutenant Dan."

Forrest is right. With or without legs, Dan Taylor is still essentially the same person. He has not lost that. But Lieutenant Dan understood a man's destiny to be fixed and fated. Now, he not only grieves the loss of his legs, but he grieves the loss of meaning and purpose to his life, which is just as bitter.

Forrest's intuitive love for his friends is matched by a similar faith. "Miracles happen every day. Some people don't think so, but they do," Forrest believes. When Lieutenant Dan rails against his fate, mocking the idea that he could walk someday in heaven, Forrest's only response is, "I'm going to heaven, Lieutenant Dan." God is not a mockery for Forrest. He is as faithful to God as he is to his friend.

Sustained by Forrest's friendship, Lieutenant Dan eventually learns to accept his new destiny. Joining Forrest in the shrimp-boat business, their nets keep coming up empty. "Where's your God now, Forrest?" Dan asks sarcastically. Forrest recollects, "Y'know, it's funny he said that, because right then, at that very moment, God showed up." God shows up in the form of a hurricane. Through the wind, waves, and rain, Dan yells out at God, "You'll never take this boat. Come on. You call this a storm? It's time for a showdown, you and me. Come and get me." When the winds subside, they are the only ship to survive the storm, and their business begins to thrive. The miracle of the filled shrimp nets changes Lieutenant Dan. On one sunny day, he turns to Forrest and says, "Forrest, I never thanked you for saving my life." Lieutenant Dan finally values his life. He has recharted his destiny. As Dan dives into the blue water and swims serenely, Forrest comments, "He never actually said so, but I think he made his peace with God."

As much as there are tragic lows in Forrest's life, there are equally high moments of good fortune and comedy. To name just a few, Forrest meets a young Elvis and influences his hip-swaying dance technique. Forrest runs onto a football field and is discovered by famed Alabama football coach Bear Bryant, who turns him into an All-American football star. Forrest is present for George Wallace's showdown against school segregation, speaks at an Abby Hoffman protest rally, and inadvertently inspires John Lennon to write the song "Imagine." He meets Presidents Kennedy, Johnson, and Nixon. He is even an eyewitness to the Watergate break-in. The serendipitous moments in *Forrest Gump* serve two purposes: they provide some needed comic relief, and they help mark significant moments in the time period—the civil rights struggle of the 1950s, the protests of the 1960s, the drug proliferation of the 1970s, and the faddishness of the 1980s.

Forrest does not need to learn any crucial life lessons throughout the course of the story. We are the ones who learn the lessons. We get to witness, through Forrest's eyes, the human tragedy of people looking for love in all the wrong places. We are able to see the truth that Mother Teresa diagnosed about human suffering:

> There is hunger for ordinary bread, and there is hunger
> for love, for kindness, for thoughtfulness; and this is the
> great poverty that makes people suffer so much.[10]

The truth is so simple, yet we, with our vaulted intelligence, constantly miss it.

In the end, the two characters closest to Forrest begin to see beyond his lack of intellect to his virtue. They realize that goodness is more valuable than worldliness; wisdom is more precious than intelligence. Both Jenny and Lieutenant Dan return to his side, which they never should have left. They had searched for answers in drugs, sexual license, and self-destructive behavior. But all they got was addiction, which only compounded their misery. The answer to the question of personal fulfillment is not in a bottle, pill, political cause, or family history. The answer cannot be reduced to an intellectual theorem. The answer is personal, not impersonal. The answer is relational, not conceptual. Love is the answer. We don't need to be a genius; we need love, gratefully received and freely given. We don't need an elite education; we need love, warmly accepted and generously offered. We don't need a Zen moment of enlightenment; we need love, humbly treasured and lavishly shared.

The Beatles sang, "All You Need Is Love." Essentially, they were right. But love is real, not an opinion formed in our minds, or merely an emotion felt in our heart. Although we can't ever fully understand the nature of love, we can know something about it. Real love belongs on the earth, in the dirt, in the day-to-day activities of real life. It is a verb—an action word—as well as a noun. It is a commitment to self-sacrifice. It is as concrete as concrete. It is more real than any movie reel. It confounds the minds of the brilliant, yet appears in the eyes of the simplest child. It embarrasses and shames; it burdens and it claims. It baptizes weary hands and sustains tired legs. It clarifies our vision and removes selfish clutter. It is the grace within the millisecond between rage and reconciliation that beckons us to forgive. Love is to die for; it is to live for.

If love is to live for, then no one exemplifies love better than Forrest's mother. Mrs. Gump knew what love really was, and she gave the real deal to her son. She is the true hero in the story. Her love centered, shielded, and guided him through the cruelties and difficulties he faced. Forrest knew he was loved, and that gave him an inner strength of character that could sustain him through anything. Forrest's life stands in contrast to an often loveless world.

When Forrest finds out that his mother is sick, he doesn't stop to contemplate the significance of the event. He drops everything and runs to her side. Corporate profits mean nothing to him compared to his mother.

"What's wrong, Momma?"
"I'm dying, Forrest. Come in and sit over here."
"Why are you dying, Momma?"

"It's my time; it's just my time. Oh, now, don't you be afraid, sweetheart. Death is just a part of life, something we are all destined to do. I didn't know it, but I was destined to be your Momma. I did the best I could."

"You did good."

"Well, I happen to believe that we make our own destiny. You have to do the best with what God gave you."

"What's my destiny, Momma?"

"You're going to have to find that out for yourself. Life is like a box of chocolates, Forrest, you never know what you're going to get."

College graduate, football All-American, Congressional Medal of Honor winner, international Ping-Pong champion, national celebrity, shrimp-boat magnate, millionaire—any one of those might suffice for the average person, but they don't have much importance for Forrest. Forrest has what the world considers success, but he still wants to know his destiny. Our destiny is found in something essential.

We were built to be bigger than our minds, so that we would not rely on our intelligence for our salvation, but rather on love. *Forrest Gump* is the story of how innocence can thrive where intelligence fails. Intelligence is not wisdom. Innocence, not intelligence, is the beginning of wisdom. Innocence is engendered by love, which reveals what is essential, and teaches us to avoid what is destructive. When anyone calls Forrest "stupid," he responds, "Stupid is as stupid does"—meaning that stupidity ought to be applied to a particular action, and not to the level of a person's intellect. By that standard, Forrest is a genius surrounded by cultural stupidity.

Forrest's silence should not be construed as shallowness of thought. When he does speak his inmost thoughts, he shows profundity and spiritual depth. When asked by Jenny about the ugliness of war, Forrest shares a moment of beauty in Vietnam and compares it to the natural beauty he has witnessed in America:

"Sometimes it would stop raining long enough for the stars to come out...and then it was nice. It was just like before the sun goes to bed down on the bayou. There is always a million sparkles on the water...like that mountain lake. It was so clear, Jenny, it looked like there were two skies, one on top of the other. And then in the desert, when the sun comes up, I couldn't tell where heaven stopped and the earth began. It's so beautiful."

"I wish I could've been there with you."

"You were."

Jenny's wounds are deeper than Lieutenant Dan's. She continues to move in and out of Forrest's life. Years later, when she learns that she is dying, she knows whom to turn to. Jenny writes to Forrest and he immediately comes to see her. To his surprise, she has a son. "You're his Daddy, Forrest." Shocked by this revelation, Forrest asks if the child is smart or slow. He doesn't want his son to be like him; he wants his son to be better than he was. When asked what he is feeling, Forrest says, "He's the most beautiful thing I've ever seen." Facing death has given Jenny the clarity to appreciate Forrest fully. He takes them home, marries Jenny, and cares for her until her death. Even if for a little time, Forrest's dream comes true.

Forrest does not let death end his relationship with Jenny. He talks to her at her grave.

Jenny, I don't know if Momma was right or it's Lieutenant Dan. I don't know if we each have a destiny or if we are just floating accidental-like on a breeze. But I think, maybe it's both. Maybe both happen at the same time. I miss you Jenny. If there's anything you need, I won't be far away.

Forrest has found a destiny more important than medals or money. He will love and raise his son, as his Momma had done for him. For a man who was deprived of a father, of normal intellect, of his beloved Jenny—he has flourished. Forrest reminds us of what is essential: love—nothing more, nothing less. Love is as love does.

Love, received from his mother and given freely to his friends, has given Forrest Gump a moral and spiritual center that enables him to glide through the turbulent times like a dolphin through the ocean, and to find the essential goodness of life. Life *is* like a box of chocolates. Although we never know what we are going to get, in whatever we get we can find sweetness.

14

Life Is Beautiful

LOVE CONQUERS ALL.

Cecchi Gori Group Miramax Films (1997)

Producers	Elda Ferri / Gianluigi Braschi
Director	Roberto Benigni
Authors of Screenplay	Vincenzo Cerami/Roberto Benigni
Running Time	118 minutes

MAIN CHARACTERS

Guido Orefice	Roberto Benigni
Dora	Nicoletta Braschi
Joshua	Giorgio Cantarini
Uncle Eliseo	Giustino Durano
Dr. Lessing	Horst Buchholz
Ferrucio	Sergio Bini Bustric

"This is a simple story, but not an easy one to tell. Like a fable, there is sorrow and, like a fable, it is full of wonder and happiness." With these words of narration, *Life Is Beautiful* begins its story of Guido Orefice and his love for his wife and child. Like a fairy tale, their love begins in wonder and light. Though darkness intrudes upon it, it does not diminish it.

The genre of *Life Is Beautiful* is unlike anything I have ever seen, a fable set in a romantic comedy. The message of love does not change, even when the tone of the story becomes considerably darker. The possibility for comedy does not change, even when the setting of the story becomes tragic. Despite the force of evil, love conquers all.

Romantic comedies often follow a simple pattern of: boy meets girl; boy loses girl; boy finds girl. But *Life Is Beautiful* takes another step: boy holds on to girl no matter how difficult life gets.

Guido is a hero, but not in the conventional sense. He is not a "pretty boy" with a sculpted body or a martial arts expert or a macho military soldier. He is not suave or sophisticated. He is, however, decent and good, armed with only his wits, charm, and humor. They are sufficient. Exemplifying these qualities, he is a most refreshing hero.

The first part of *Life Is Beautiful* is primarily a storybook romance. Guido, a humble waiter, meets Dora, who drops out of the sky and into his arms. She is the woman of his dreams, who is begrudgingly betrothed to another man. With comedy and cleverness, Guido sets out to win her for his own.

By clever improvisation, a mark of this romantic comedy, Guido slowly wins the heart of Dora and rescues her from her fascist suitor. During a party to announce her engagement, Dora beckons Guido to meet her under the banquet table, where their eyes lock, and Dora says, "Take me away!" As if in a fairy tale, Guido reenters the banquet gallantly riding a horse into her engagement party to rescue his fair maiden in distress. They are married and are destined to live happily ever after in love, were it not for the hatred of others.

Throughout the humorous scenes, there are ominous hints of trouble. Italy in 1939 was beset with fascism and anti-Semitism, and they slowly intrude upon the lives of Guido, a Jew, and Dora, a Gentile. For example, in the opening comedic scene, Guido and his friend Ferrucio are speeding down a hill in a car with no brakes, toward a group of onlookers who are waiting for a fascist political official to drive by. Guido stands up in his car seat and gestures for them to move, parodying a Nazi salute, which they return. There are other signs as well, as when Guido's uncle's horse is painted green and labeled a "Jewish horse," or when Guido presents a mocking speech to schoolchildren on racial supremacy. The scenes are humorous, but the events foreshadow darkness yet to come.

Life Is Beautiful is an island in a sea of inane romantic comedies that equate love with feelings. When everything goes our way, feelings of romantic love are easy to have. But as the setting of the story begins to change, Guido's love remains. Romantic love, or any kind of love for that matter, is not a feeling. Although it includes feelings, love is an act of the will, a commitment made for the spiritual growth of another; it is sacrifice and an attitude of service toward the beloved. Before Guido starts a day at work as a waiter, his boss instructs him, "You're serving. You're not a servant. Serving is a supreme art. God is the first servant. God serves men but he is not a servant to men." In our loving service to others, we mirror the very work of God.

The second part of the film begins after several years have passed, on the birthday of Guido and Dora's five-year-old son, Joshua. Again, romantic comedies today rarely involve children as important characters. Most usually end in romance. Joshua, however, is not an intrusion into Guido and Dora's love; he is the fulfillment of it. Romantic love finds its fruition in familial love. God providing, one matures into the other.

Despite the hardships caused by the political persecution of the Jews, Guido, Dora, and their son maintain a happy life. But the political climate in Italy worsens. The Jews are ordered to be rounded up for internment in concentration camps. Guido and Joshua are loaded onto a train whose tracks lead to death.

Dora, being a Gentile, is not forced onto the train, yet she chooses to board anyway. Whether prudent or not, her decision is a powerful symbol. She wishes to be near her husband and child and to share in their ordeal. For Dora, loving Guido and Joshua means service to them. Though not a Jew, like Ruth she chooses to be counted as one of them.

To find ugliness in beauty is a great crime. To find beauty in ugliness is the mark of a saint. The fascists saw ugliness in Jewish beauty. Guido and Dora's love was beauty that they shared amid the ugliness of hate.

As the setting turns to life in the concentration camp, Guido is determined to shield his son as best he can from the terrifying reality of the situation. He concocts a fantastic story for Joshua, telling him that the train ride and camp are all part of an elaborate game. The object is to endure the camp and be the first father-son team to collect one thousand points. The winner gets a real tank. He convinces Joshua that the guards are not really angry. The game will involve hide-and-seek and silence, which Guido really uses to keep Joshua alive. By deflecting and laughing off Joshua's most serious concerns (such as the rumor that they are going to be killed and turned into "buttons and soap"), Guido manages to shield Joshua from the grim reality that surrounds him and makes it seem like a vacation.

Why does Guido go to all that trouble? Because he is a father who loves his son; therefore, he is mindful not only of Joshua's body but also of his spirit. Guido not only fears for Joshua's life, he also fiercely tries to protect his innocence as well. If he can, Guido wants to save his child's capacity for wonder, love, and faith. These are treasures five-year-olds have, as do some adults like Guido. Despite knowing full well that the web of enchantment he has spun around Joshua could be broken at any minute, he nonetheless uses every ounce of energy that is left in his tired body to preserve Joshua's life and the interior life of his soul.

Guido guards Joshua's innocence as preciously as he guards his life. Parents shield their children from evil; it's what God calls us to do. Exhausted and starving from carrying anvils in work details, Guido never stops trying to be a father to Joshua. Saint Augustine said, "He who says he has done enough has already perished." By loving Joshua, Guido makes possible for Joshua, too, to learn to live an attitude of love. He teaches love by loving.

Joshua is sheltered from much of the brutal realities around him by his loving father. Because of this, he will have few nightmares that could torment him. Instead, they will be replaced by memories of his father's love. Thus, the story is a twentieth-century parable of a father who loves his child beyond human understanding, who shelters his child from evil, who hallows his innocence.

Life Is Beautiful is a celebration of the value of childhood—for children and adults. Peter Pan was right not to want grow up into the vices of adulthood, but wrong not to grow. Perhaps we are called to "grow toward" God. To do so, we must rediscover the childlike virtues of wonder, respect, faith, and love. This is not an option; it's a necessity. "Unless you change and become like children, you will never enter the kingdom of heaven," Jesus warned (Matt 18:3). The definition of adulthood ought to be "one who is skilled in the virtues of childhood." Guido is a beautiful illustration of how fathers must be childlike in order to save their children. Saint Thérèse of Lisieux wrote, "The little way is the way of spiritual childhood, the way of trust and surrender. To remain little means recognizing one's nothingness, expecting everything from the good God as a little child expects everything from his father." Thérèse did not know it, but she has provided us with an excellent character description of Guido.

Even though they are separated into different camps, Guido still finds a way to express his love for Dora. While serving the camp officials as a waiter, Guido discovers a phonograph record of "their song," which he broadcasts through the camp speaker system. Dora hears the love song, from an opera by the Jewish composer Offenbach, and rises from her bed. She stares out into the night sky. They are unable to see or touch each other, but it doesn't matter. For a precious moment, they are together again—united in love.

Guido is able to keep his capacity for cleverness and humor in the camp, despite the oppressive circumstances. To make that believable within the confines of the story, the camp is depicted in a less realistic way than was actual life in a concentration camp. In response, some critics have attacked the movie for belittling the Holocaust. But they are not correct. The film has the opposite effect. We must remember that we are watching an adult fable. The graphic and gruesome details of the camp, as seen in historical documentaries, are so horrific that they can seem unreal to us. But because *Life Is Beautiful* does not have them, we are able to experience the human tragedy through Guido and Dora in a very personal way. We do not need our fables to be real; we need them to be true.

Guido's first hope for some way out of the concentration camp comes when he is brought to a medical inspection. To his surprise, Dr. Lessing is conducting it. The German Dr. Lessing had been a favorite customer of Guido's at the restaurant. They would entertain each other with riddles. Dr. Lessing had left Guido with this one: "Once you say my name, I am no longer there. Who am I?" Dr. Lessing, who is looking only at bodies, not persons, barely notices him, until Guido says, "Silence"—the answer to the riddle.

Dr. Lessing agrees to meet Guido later in private, but when they finally meet, Dr. Lessing whispers to him,

> Fat fat, ugly ugly,
> all yellow in reality.
> If you ask me what I am
> I answer "cheap, cheap, cheap."
> Walking along I go "poopoo,"
> who am I, tell me true?

"Help me, for heaven's sake, Guido. I can't even sleep." All Dr. Lessing is interested in is having Guido help him with a stupid riddle. Guido can only stare back at Lessing for a moment, unable to believe that he could care only about a riddle when Guido cares about the survival of his wife and child. Dr. Lessing doesn't want to help; he wants to be helped. With starvation, disease, turmoil, and murder all around him, he can only think of himself. Lessing is the perfect example of self-insulation and self-centeredness; he personifies what is wrong with the Nazi mentality. Lessing is in "pain" as people are slaughtered around him. Rather than see their pain and be compelled to act for them, he shuts himself in himself and deals with his riddles. He has reduced life to a mental problem to be solved, and with that he has begun a mental breakdown. Lessing receives no answer to the riddle, just as he has no answer to the riddle of his own existence.

"Silence" is a theme that runs throughout *Life Is Beautiful*. Early on, when Guido asks his uncle why he did not cry out against his attackers, Uncle Eliseo tells him, "Silence is the most powerful cry." "Silence" is the answer to one of Dr. Lessing's riddles. In the camp, Joshua must play the "silence game" in order to survive. Sadly, after trying to find Dora in order to liberate her from the camp, there is only the silence of death after Guido is murdered by machine gun fire.

Guido's death is unseen but felt by the viewer. Without ever showing the blood, we feel the loss. Guido made the world around him more bearable. Throughout the story, his fortune may have changed, but Guido never does. Whether the circumstances were fortuitous or dangerous, he remained himself. He looked to find the good in every situation, every moment being a potential opportunity to love Dora or Joshua. While there is still life, there is the freedom to choose our attitude. Guido chose love. "I know of only one duty," Albert Camus wrote, "and that is to love."

In an act of wrongly used power, we lower our humanity, not raise it. In an act of service, we raise our humanity, not lower it. He who plays the clown is a prince. For Guido, noticing that his son is safely hidden and watching him, even the march to his death is an opportunity to make his son laugh. If even for a brief moment there is life; there is an opportunity for love and laughter.

In the final narration, Joshua says, "This is my story. This was his gift to me—this was his sacrifice." What was the gift?—certainly, the gift of life. Guido's ingenuity saves Joshua from certain death. But there was a deeper gift given as well. By protecting his child's innocence, Guido not only gave him life, but he also preserved his capacity to see that "life is beautiful." Therein lies the meaning behind the title. *La Vita e bella* is the attitude Guido has toward life because he chose to love and be loved. Circumstance does not alter it. A fable could have no better truth to tell.

Roberto Benigni, who portrays Guido and also directed and co-wrote the film, said that the title came from a quote by Leon Trotsky. When barricaded in his Mexican compound for fear that he was about to be killed by one of Stalin's assassins, he saw his wife in the courtyard and wrote in a letter that, in spite of everything "life is beautiful."

Life *is* beautiful because it was made by love. Love made us, and love makes us still. Death cannot diminish its presence. In the end, when we stand before God, God will command of us, "Tell me of how you loved and whom you loved." Love is all we are responsible for. Without love, Saint Paul said, "I am nothing" (1 Cor 13:2). Mother Teresa said,

> The greatest disease in the West today is not TB or leprosy: it is being unwanted, unloved, and uncared for. We can cure physical diseases with medicine, but the only cure for loneliness, despair, and hopelessness is love. There are many people dying for a piece of bread but there are many more dying for a little love. The poverty in the West is a different kind of poverty—it is not only a poverty of loneliness but also of spirituality. There's a hunger for love, as there is a hunger for God.[11]

At the end of the film, after the camp is liberated, Joshua is reunited with his mother. After getting a ride in an American tank, Joshua embraces her and declares, "We won!" They had won. Guido's deepest hope had been fulfilled. Dora and Joshua were alive. His sacrificial love had brought them together again. Love always wins over hate. Whether we see that victory in this life or the next, love always wins. Joshua was right. Through love, they *had* won. Love conquers all.

15

The Truman Show

BE NOT CONFORMED TO THIS WORLD.

Paramount Pictures (1998)

Producer	Edward S. Feldman
Director	Peter Weir
Author of Screenplay	Andrew Niccol
Running Time	103 minutes

MAIN CHARACTERS

Truman Burbank	Jim Carrey
Meryl	Laura Linney
Marlon	Noah Emmerich
Lauren/Sylvia	Natascha McElhone
Christof	Ed Harris

Some sing, "And I think to myself, what a wonderful world." Others sing, "Stop the world, I want to get off." The world is a paradox. On the one hand, it is created by God in original grace, and therefore each person, place, and thing is good in itself and points beyond itself to the greater glory of God. On the other hand, with original sin, there abounds evil in the world that can entice us to the lesser vainglory of self. It is to the latter of which Saint John's letters warns. He warns us not to love the things of the world—

war, retribution, arrogance, and so forth—in other words, that aspect of the world that has rejected Christ (1 John 2:15). To do otherwise would be our own curse. If we love that world, we lose the capacity to see it as it really is. If we love the things of this world more than persons or God, it is personhood itself that will be assaulted. In the end, if we love things, we will see ourselves as things and be treated like things.

The same paradox exists in culture as well and in the art it engenders. Art is an important thing. Art is a reflection of truth. Its noble purpose is to inspire the soul and illuminate our humanity. But what if the art world no longer served this purpose and instead saw itself as its own master? What if art, unconstrained by moral law, became more important than the individual? Art, no longer for humanity's sake, would become art for art's sake. Artists would become like Narcissus transfixed only by the sight of their own image. The result would be that popular art would be hailed as more valuable than the populace, and the human person would be reduced to the status of a thing. In short, George Orwell's prophesied "Big Brother" would turn out not to be the government, as he had warned, but the Hollywood art world. What would we do? What would a "true man" do? Such is the subject of an imaginative film called *The Truman Show,* with Truman's extraordinary circumstances being far closer to the existential human condition than we might suspect.

The Truman Show follows the sheltered life of Truman Burbank, played by Jim Carrey. Truman is the unwitting star of a twenty-four-hour-a-day, nonstop documentary soap opera. Since his birth and adoption by a media megacorporation, over five-thousand concealed cameras have broadcast every moment of Truman's life to a worldwide audience. Unbeknown to him, his friends and family are actors. Even his hometown island of Seahaven is an elaborate studio set enclosed in a giant dome, complete with high-tech simulations of sun, moon, and sky. He is a prisoner in a made-for-TV paradise. Like a puppet on a string for more than thirty years, Truman is trapped in a surreal prison not of his own making, with the unseen hand of Christof, the show's architect and producer, continually manufacturing ways to keep Truman on the island. Christof, a delusional lord of Hollywood played by Ed Harris, cares about ratings, not about Truman. He gives the public what they want and justifies his actions by professing, "I have given Truman the chance to live a normal life. The world, the place you live in, is the sick place. Seahaven is the way the world should be.... Truman prefers his cell." Despite the darkly comic setting of this story, its message is ultimately inspiring. The Truman Show is really the story of his escape, for a "true man" can have no strings to hold him down.

Despite Christof's malevolent control over Truman's world, a series of events occurs that reveals to Truman that there is something more than the confines of Seahaven: a stage light falls to earth from out of a clear blue sky; a downpour of rain falls only on him; he hears a radio broadcast that recounts his every move; and he encounters his long-lost father, only to have him abruptly taken away by mysterious strangers. Truman's limited world can provide no reasonable explanation for these phenomena. They point to a world beyond his own, another reality beyond what his senses have previously experienced. Truman courageously begins to act on his suspicions, despite the world around him trying to convince him to ignore this impulse and settle for the pleasure, convenience, security, and comfort of his known world. Every time he ventures forth to see if there is more to his life, the people around him pull him back to the day-to-day details. Truman is a slave to Christof. He is betrayed by his pseudofamily and friends that take advantage of his bond of trust with them. They persuade him to forget his wanderlust and be satisfied that Seahaven is all there is. But Truman remains true to himself and continues his quest to find the meaning of his own existence. In doing so, Truman lives out a calling given to us all.

Truman's choice is essentially the same as ours. Will we prefer comfortable illusions offered to us or the painful truth? Unlike Truman's counterfeit world, the physical world is a grace. Although our world, unlike Truman's counterfeit world, displays authentic beauty and love, it does have its limitations. We all seek a joy that this world cannot satisfy.

Every human being has experiences that point to realities beyond what our senses can grasp. Confident that the visible, tangible world doesn't have all the answers, many people respond to God's invitation to walk in faith. But to the extent that the secular culture becomes more hostile to authentic religious life, it will become increasingly difficult for us to trust in God. The most dangerous secular message given today is that our world is all there is and that we may as well settle for the pleasure, convenience, security, and comfort that it offers. Television, the Internet, billboards, radio, and magazines bombard us with messages that promote a culture of materialism and narcissism. As Saint Augustine said, "Sin is believing the lie that you are self-centered, self-dependent, and self-contained."

The materialist, like the characters in *The Truman Show,* will explain away every "clue" of another world. Does the design in the universe point to an ultimate Designer? No, we are told; we are just a random accident. Does our quest for the meaning of existence point to a God who has a purpose and a plan for all of creation? No, they scoff; just grab pleasure while we can. As the producer Christof cynically states, "We accept the realities of the world we are presented. It's that simple." But Christof is as wrong about Truman as he is about us. Courageously, men and women of faith refuse to accept that this is all there is.

For Truman, the key event beyond all the other signs that most profoundly affects him is his encounter with Sylvia. For a few short moments, one cast member breaks the staged illusion and genuinely shows love to Truman. She tells him the truth. For the first time in his life, Truman experiences a glimpse of real love. Once Christof becomes aware that she is spoiling the illusion, he immediately has her taken away. But the damage has been done; the spell has been broken. The effect of the love remains. "They got rid of her," a barmaid explains, "but they couldn't erase the memory." Truman can't forget Sylvia or her last words to him as she was taken away: "Get out of here. Come and find me." With ritual care, he reconstructs an image of her to keep her memory alive. It took someone on the outside of Truman's world to break inside, to reveal to him the truth. It is the same with us.

The ordinary world is full of signs of the existence of God. But the key event that affected humanity was the Christ-event. For a few brief years in human history, the eternal God inserted himself into human history and demonstrated genuine love to us. From that point on and forever, we have the ultimate glimpse of divine love. Once the religious establishment of his time became aware that Jesus was threatening their power, they had him eliminated. But truth is stronger than fiction, love stronger than death. The effect of the love remains. Christ asks us to come and follow him. With ritual care we reconstruct the image of his cross to keep alive the memory of his death and his victory over it.

Truman is faced with an ultimate decision—illusion or truth. He must abandon everything and everyone who has helped to spin the web of deceit that entraps him—cultural norms, career, best friend, wife, even his family—and transcend them. He has to take a voyage of faith. Fearlessly, Truman risks it all, even his life, to find the truth of his existence. Realizing that pleasure will no longer imprison Truman, Christof plays God with Truman's life. Using the technological wizardry at his disposal, he tries to kill Truman. He would rather have Truman dead than the truth revealed. But the human spirit is stronger than death, and Truman is triumphant.

Although Truman's fictional circumstances are pretty far-fetched, we are confronted with essentially the same choice. Our choice does not ask us to hide from the culture or to deny the genuine good within it, but only to break free of any illusions with which we are confronted.

Faith comes down to an ultimate decision, one that will chart the course of our lives. We must abandon everything and everyone—cultural norms, career, best friends, and spouses, even family—that prevent God from being the *summum bonum,* the highest good, in our lives. One's whole heart, soul, and strength must be directed toward God. Like Truman, we must take the voyage of faith. We have to be willing to risk it all to discover the truth of our existence. We are not asked to surrender mere comfort; we are asked to surrender our very self.

When we love another person, we gain a perspective beyond our own personal limits. We get out of our own way. And wisdom increases clarity, as binoculars (two eyes using two lenses) allow us a greater perception of reality than a spyglass (one eye using two lenses). Each person offers a unique angle on life. The more we love others, the more we can see the world through other people's eyes. The more "lenses" the better. Thus, our capacity to love is directly related to our facility to know the truth of our own existence. When we increase love, we inversely decrease self-centered illusion. As in a nautical voyage, the more points of reference a navigator can have the better he can determine his proper position. On our voyage of faith, the more points of personal reference we can encounter in acts of authentic love, the better we can determine our proper spiritual position in life.

This is a lesson that Truman must learn. He must courageously lose the comforts of his world in order to gain the truth. In order to gain real love in the next world, embodied in his romantic love for Sylvia, he must forsake the illusions in his own world. And he does. This is the essence of the Christian message. We must courageously choose love in order to gain the truth. In order to gain real love, embodied in the person of Jesus Christ, we must forsake our world's illusions.

The architects of cultural narcissism insist that we are the center, even if, in fact, we are not. Christof tries to convince Truman of this lie when he says, "There is no more truth out there than there is in the world I have created for you. Same lies, same deceit." But ultimately, no one can quell the supernatural longing that dwells inside each person. As Aldous Huxley wrote, "There comes a time when a man asks, even of Shakespeare, even of Beethoven, is this all?" The Christian answer to Huxley's question is a delightful, "there is more. There is much more." As good as life gets, this life is not as good as it gets. We are made for more. We were made for forever. Our entire life is merely the introduction to the book of human existence. Chapter one, the real beginning, awaits us.

Some might find the plot of *The Truman Show* farfetched and an unrealistic metaphor for our situation. They believe that Hollywood would never stoop so low as to exploit or enslave a person, merely for ratings. Really? Although the circumstances in *The Truman Show* are extraordinarily dark, the premise is not far from reality. Tabloid-driven talk shows daily exploit the miseries of people, offering them an hour of fame in exchange for publicly parading their dysfunctional relationships. Movie producers exploit Jews, women, Catholics, and African Americans (to name a few) if it suits the success and profitability of their films. Top-rated shock-jocks demean women for listening pleasure so regularly that they can hardly be called "shocking" anymore. Time-Warner sells rap CDs that celebrate "cop killing." Exploitation done in the name of art is commonplace. CBS recruits contestants to trade their honor and self-respect for prize money on so-called "reality" shows like *Survivor*. (An ironic name, for their souls rarely survive the experience without damage.) From art to politics, the corrupt harvest people like a crop for consumption. They ride people as if they were an amusement park attraction and then dispose of them when they've got their money's worth. Like the power-drunk movie producer Christof, media moguls make or break reputations with their morning coffee.

In the face of the narcissistic delusions that Christians see around them, there is reason to be hopeful. Hope sees beyond the data our minds can gather to the promise our hearts can fathom. No matter how hard those cultural forces of our age try to suppress the basic religious impulse, they cannot keep a true man or true woman down. Evil already tried and failed to suppress Christ who was the "true Man." Evil will fail again. Deprive humans of spiritual food and we only get hungrier. Tell us enough lies and we will revolt in search of the truth. Unlike Truman, we don't have to leave the culture, just transcend its limitations. Our task is not to leave our Seahavens, but rather, to interact with and engage the culture with the good news that we can all find a true haven in God.

16

Les Misérables

LOVE IS ABOVE THE LAW.

Mandalay Entertainment /
Columbia Pictures (1998)

Producer	James Gorman
Director	Bille August
Author of Screenplay	Rafael Yglesias
Running Time	134 minutes

MAIN CHARACTERS

Jean Valjean	Liam Neeson
Inspector Javert	Geoffrey Rush
Fantine	Uma Thurman
Cosette	Claire Danes
Marius	Hans Matheson

Les Misérables is a tale of two cities—the city of God versus the city of humankind. Jean Valjean is the citizen who embodies the virtue of love and its qualities of mercy and forgiveness. Inspector Javert is the citizen who embodies the vice of cruelty that results from the sins of pride and self-righteousness. Valjean knows compassion; Javert knows only his brand of justice. Valjean believes in a love that transcends law; Javert believes in a law that judges others.

Les Misérables takes place at the turn of the eighteenth century in France, but its message is timeless and boundless. The film version is an adaptation of the famous story by Victor Hugo. Because of the story's immense scope and detail, the 1998 film version cuts much of the early portion of the story and begins with Jean Valjean's moment of grace.

Jean Valjean is a paroled and bitter man, convinced of the cruelty of all humanity and the God who made them. Paroled felons were required by law to carry identification at all times. But no innkeeper would accept a dangerous felon. Unable to find food or lodging, Valjean finally finds shelter with a priest, who generously provides him with bread, wine, and a bed. "How do you know I won't kill you?" he asks the priest. "How do you know I won't kill *you?* I suppose we will have to trust each other," the priest responds. But food and lodging for a night do not undo nineteen years of hard labor. Valjean steals the priest's sterling silverware and flees, but is caught by the gendarmes and returned in chains to the priest's home.

The priest is within his legal rights to have Valjean imprisoned. Instead, he exclaims to Valjean, "Why didn't you take the candlesticks!" The priest denies the theft and places the silver candlesticks within Valjean's sack. Valjean is exonerated of the crime. He can only stare back in disbelief. Mercy and forgiveness bestowed on a convict? The priest places his hands on Valjean's shoulders and proclaims:

> Don't forget. Don't ever forget that you've promised to become a new man. Jean Valjean, my brother, you no longer belong to evil. With this silver, I've bought your soul. I've ransomed you from fear and hatred. Now I give you back to God.

One powerful act of forgiveness breaks the quarried stone that had surrounded Valjean's heart. For him, it is as if he has been baptized in the River Jordan. In his moment of repentance, the weight of hate is lifted off his shoulders—the dirt of nineteen years finally washed clean. He has been re-created, reborn. With this act of love from the priest, Valjean can no longer believe that all humankind and God are wicked. The unstolen mercy and forgiveness he received from the priest, he would now direct to his fellow creatures.

In Alexander Dumas' *The Count of Monte Cristo,* Edmond Dantes' encounter with a saintly priest gives him earthly power, which he uses for revenge. In Victor Hugo's *Les Misérables,* Jean Valjean's encounter with a saintly priest gives him holiness, which he uses for service to others. Although it is a parole violation, he leaves behind his old identity and begins again. The story continues nine years later when Valjean's transformation of the heart has led to a fortuitous transformation in his circumstances. Having risen from factory worker to factory owner, his humane and dignified treatment of his workers resulted in the townsfolk insisting on his becoming mayor. Jean Valjean, the dangerous convict, has become Monsieur Madeleine, the gentleman mayor of the town of Vigau.

Valjean had reluctantly agreed, being ever mindful of his criminal identity. Nonetheless, he was able to keep his past a secret until Javert, a former guard at the prison quarries of Toulon, where Valjean had been an inmate, arrives in Vigau as the new police inspector.

Police inspector Javert is a man of discipline and procedure, a man who abides by the law. The law is his salvation. He cannot see the tragedy of prostitution, only its criminality. In his twisted mind, his obedience to the law gives him the power to make personal judgments. It justifies his personal disdain for his own parents (his father was a thief and his mother a prostitute), and allows Javert to act with cruelty toward criminals.

When a heavy cart accidentally falls on one of the factory workers, Valjean immediately lifts the enormous weight off the employee's injured body. Witnessing the display, Javert remembers Valjean's strength at the prison and recognizes him. Once a criminal, always a criminal, Javert believes. He begins to seek the proof he needs to expose Valjean. When Valjean asks him whether a prisoner could reform his life, Javert explains: "Reform is a discredited fantasy. Modern science tells us that people are by nature law breakers or law abiders. A wolf can wear sheep's clothing but he's still a wolf."

But according to Christ, we are all sheep—lost sheep. A lost sheep is not a wolf. This is not to say that we can ignore wolflike thoughts or behavior. It is to say that we are not in a position to label anyone a wolf. To be more precise, our faith teaches us to judge ideas as true or false, actions as good or evil, but never to judge a person as essentially noble or wretched, worthy or unworthy, saved or damned. That judgment is for God alone to make. We hate the sin, not the sinner. We judge the action, not the person. Javert's scientific determinism has given him license to make personal judgments dispensed with cruelty. He sees himself as a man of truth and justice. But it is literal truth and legal justice, with no allowance for love.

Preoccupied by the arrival of Javert and the threat he poses, Valjean is unaware that one of his employees, a woman named Fantine, has been publicly exposed for having a child out of wedlock. Despite being desperate to earn money for the boarding of her six-year-old daughter, Cosette, Fantine is dismissed. Javert's narrow cruelty is turned on Fantine, who has been forced into prostitution. Though she is weak and ill, Javert tortures her and sentences her to prison. When Valjean finally finds out what has happened to her, he rushes to her aid. He orders her released and brings her to his home. As the priest had once cared for him, Valjean cares for Fantine. But her tuberculosis is too advanced. She is dying. He apologizes to her:

> "I was preoccupied. I didn't know."
> "I'm a whore and Cosette has no father."
> "She has the Lord. He is her Father. And you are his creation. In his eyes, you have never been anything but an innocent and beautiful woman."

Valjean promises to care for Cosette. But to make matters worse for him, he discovers that an innocent man is standing trial accused of being Jean Valjean. Valjean's capacity for mercy extends to the innocent man accused. He stands up at the trial and declares, "I am Jean Valjean! I wish I could keep my mouth shut but I cannot." By admitting his real identity, he becomes a fugitive once again.

Transferring ownership of his company to his employees, Valjean finds refuge for himself and Cosette in a convent in Paris. Javert pursues him but is legally unable to enter past the convent wall. He takes up a position as chief inspector in Paris, hoping someday to arrest Valjean.

When Cosette turns seventeen, she longs to see the outside world. Unable to keep her completely sheltered anymore, Valjean moves with Cosette into a Paris home. He finances a charity that offers soup and clothing to the poor. He offers food so that others will not have to resort to crime as he did many years ago. While assisting Valjean, Cosette falls in love with a student radical named Marius, who speaks out against the government, "Being poor is the worst crime of all. And if you commit this crime, you are condemned for life." Marius speaks out publicly for justice, as Valjean quietly fights for it through charity. Being a dangerous revolutionary, Marius draws the attention of Javert.

Cosette is torn between love for her father and love for Marius. With Javert closing in, Jean Valjean reveals to Cosette the truth.

> I am a convict. When I was young, just your age, I was very poor. I was starving. One day, I stood in front of a window. A window full of bread. There was just glass between me and not being hungry anymore. It was so easy. So I broke it and took what I wanted. Then they caught me and put me in chains for almost twenty years. They did things to me—I can't tell you about it. And I did things, there in the jail. Terrible things. I became an animal. They took my dignity. They took everything from me.

When Javert discovers Valjean's identity in Paris, he closes in to capture the one who has eluded him for so long. In order to make the arrest, Javert goes into an area of town that is temporarily occupied by Marius and his fellow revolutionaries. Here, Javert is captured by the revolutionaries and is given over to Valjean for execution. The roles have reversed.

From a moral point of view, Javert is guilty as charged. He had made Valjean a fugitive, brutally mistreated Fantine, and would have killed Cosette's lover. "You should kill me. I won't stop. I won't let you go," Javert tells Valjean. With gun in hand, Valjean takes Javert into a back alley. Valjean takes aim, and fires—upward. The hunted sets free his hunter. He shows Javert a mercy that Javert had never shown him. The merciless judge had been granted a reprieve. Javert's ordered world of judgment and law begins to crumble.

Mercy to his injured worker, to Fantine, to the innocent man accused, to the poor of Paris, and now, mercy to one who least deserves it—Javert. Valjean is the example of Christ's command, "But I say to you, Love your enemies and pray for those who persecute you" (Matt 5:44). Valjean is the Christian hero. He has found love and forgiveness in God. To receive forgiveness, he must dispense it—even to those who least deserve it. "As we forgive those who trespass against us."

Jean Valjean's capacity for mercy confuses Javert. He understands only law and justice. But there exists something more than the law: love. It does not ignore justice; it upholds it and rises beyond it.

In the end, Valjean displays sacrificial love by offering himself to Javert as ransom in exchange for letting Marius go free. Javert has finally won. He shackles Valjean near the River Seine. But his mind is troubled. Before taking him in to prison, he asks Valjean:

> "Why didn't you kill me?"
> "I don't have the right to kill you."
> "But you hate me?"
> "I don't hate you. I don't feel anything."
> "You don't want to go back to the [prison], do you?
> Then, for once, we agree."

Javert places the barrel of the gun to Valjean's head.

"I'm going to spare you from a life in prison, Jean Valjean. It's a pity that rules don't allow me to be merciful. I've tried to live my life without breaking a single rule—You're free."

Unexpectedly, Javert grants Valjean his freedom. Somehow, by the grace of God, his heart had led him to perform an act of charity his mind could not fully comprehend or live with. He had always lived by the law. Now, he was in violation of it. Violators must be punished. Shackling himself in his own chains, Javert falls back into the River Seine and drowns himself. He could not live above the law. He lived by the law and he died by it.

Like Valjean's encounter with the priest years earlier, Javert had experienced a moment of grace. But he could not let go of what he believed about the law. To do so would judge his entire life a travesty. Death was easier than admitting the lie he had lived. Javert had said, "An honest man has nothing to fear from the truth." But he had never been honest with himself. Therefore, the law that had chained him his entire life would bring about his demise.

Could law be so misused and misunderstood? It was by some Pharisees at the time of Christ. They had misused the law to justify pride. Law became a spiritual prison in which they were locked, unable or unwilling to see the damaging effect it was having on their souls. For them, and just as much for us, Jesus offered the new law.

In his Sermon on the Mount, found in one of the most challenging chapters in all of scripture, Matthew 5, Jesus proclaims the new law that would demand, not *more* from us, but *the most* from us. The new law was an addition, not a subtraction:

Do not think that I have come to abolish the law or the prophets; I have come not to abolish but to fulfill.... Therefore, whoever breaks one of the least of these commandments, and teaches others to do the same, will be called least in the kingdom of heaven; but whoever does them and teaches them will be called great in the kingdom of heaven. (Matt 5:17, 19)

Going above the letter of the law, Jesus calls for obedience to its spirit. He reversed our expectations on who is truly blessed in the eyes of God. He called *blessed* the poor in spirit, the mournful, the meek, the just, the merciful, the pure, and the peacemaker. Because they live in humility, God can live in them.

And to those who might think in their pride and self-righteousness that they had fulfilled the law and were therefore superior, Jesus raised the legal bar as high above them as God himself. We had been commanded not to kill; now we must not show vengeance. We had been commanded not to commit adultery; now we must not have a lustful thought. We had been allowed to divorce; now we must honor our marital vows. We had been commanded to love our neighbor; now we must love our enemy. In short, we must "be perfect, therefore, as your heavenly Father is perfect" (Matt 5:48).

It is a law none of us can follow perfectly. None of us can afford the illusion of self-righteousness. Jesus' teaching would not allow for any superiority. The new law is more than mere law; it is an attitude of humility, the fertile soil necessary for real faith and love to grow. Jesus set the standard so high because God's standards are high—higher than legalistic followers wanted to believe. They hadn't earned salvation by fulfilling the law. They can't fulfill the law perfectly, because they aren't perfect.

The New Testament recounts the story of another man who was shackled by the righteousness of the law. But for the apostle Paul, his spiritual death was a rebirth in Christ. Paul had been a Pharisee who persecuted the early Christians because their beliefs were in violation of Judaic law. But after his encounter with the risen Christ on the road to Damascus, Paul came to understand that we cannot earn our way to salvation by adhering to the letter of the law. Christ's death and resurrection had set us free from the debt of sin, enabling us to receive the free gift of salvation. We are saved, not because we have earned our worthiness, but because God has made us worthy. Saint Paul wrote, "But now we are discharged from the law, dead to that which held us captive, so that we are slaves not under the old written code but in the new life of the Spirit" (Rom 7:6).

For pseudoreligious people the law has been a safe ship in a storm, but it is really a prison barge, as it was for Javert. We cannot misuse it to give ourselves the illusion of propriety and superiority before others. We cannot earn salvation. Jean Valjean acted with love out of gratitude for a love that had been shown him by the priest. We must act with love out of gratitude for a love that has been shown us by God through Jesus Christ. Paul understood this when he wrote, "Owe no one anything, except to love one another; for the one who loves another has fulfilled the law" (Rom 13:8).

Justice must be served. And love must serve. Beyond justice, we are commanded to love. Mercy and forgiveness are the qualities of love. In that dynamic of love, we will find God and our happiness. Love exists above the law.

17

Harry Potter and the Sorcerer's Stone

BECOME LIKE A CHILD.

1492 Pictures / Warner Brothers (2001)

Producer	David Heyman
Director	Chris Columbus
Author of Screenplay	Steven Kloves
Running Time	152 minutes

MAIN CHARACTERS

Harry Potter	Daniel Radcliffe
Hermione Granger	Emma Watson
Ron Weasley	Rupert Grint
Albus Dumbledore	Richard Harris
Rubeus Hagrid	Robbie Coltrane

What next should we expect from the children of today? Will they be storming the grocery stores requesting broccoli and cauliflower? Will children across America start meticulously cleaning their bedrooms? Perhaps they will. Hell may not have frozen over, but it may have lowered a bit in temperature. A few years ago, we could never imagine kids, even as young as eight years of age, voluntarily reading a series of books that eventually were more than seven-hundred-pages long—and liking them. Yet that is exactly what has been happening in countless families beginning in the late 1990s. All of this craziness is occurring without teachers assigning the books or parents demanding reading time. It is almost as if a magic spell has been cast over the children of the world. One has. It comes from the wand of English author J. K. Rowling, and it has to do with a most unlikely hero, a boy named Harry Potter.

Harry Potter came to life in the mind of J. K. Rowling on a long train ride from Manchester to London. By the time the trip was over, she had outlined much of the basic story, which was to become *Harry Potter and the Sorcerer's Stone*. Harry Potter is a fictional breath of fresh air. From the start, he possessed none of the qualities of "cool" that are so marketed to young people today. Harry is a wobbly-kneed boy who wears broken glasses. Far from designer clothes, he wears oversized hand-me-downs from his obnoxious cousin. He doesn't own a computer or video games, doesn't participate in club activities, and is constantly bullied. He longs for his parents, rather than finding it fashionable to be alienated from them. Because he is the antithesis of the typical "cool" kid, Harry has an unusual value to his fans. *Harry Potter and the Sorcerer's Stone* is the story of one boy's magical destiny with greatness.

Why has the "hero of Hogwarts" taken such an incredible hold over young people? Harry Potter is every kid's deepest wish come true: that no matter how tragic or commonplace the circumstances of their lives, no matter how mundane and average they are made to feel, they, like Harry, are *special*. They are destined for great things.

Unbeknown to most of its readers and viewers, Harry Potter serves to reveal the very nature of the human person that lies at the core of Christian teaching. Human beings *are* special. We are created in the image and likeness of God. We each have a supernatural destiny and are here for a reason. Life, as it is in *Harry Potter,* is an adventure with the promise of a happy ending, no matter how unhappy our beginnings may have been.

Rowling has gone to great lengths to ensure that the movie version is faithful to the story that first gave life to Harry Potter.

Directed by Chris Columbus and released in 2001, the movie strays very little from the literary story line. Potter fans would have it no other way.

For both the book and subsequent film, much of the success of *Harry Potter and the Sorcerer's Stone* goes to Rowling's witty prose style and the imaginative world she creates for her readers. But beyond that, *Harry Potter* is not so much profound as it is good fun, in the best sense of the phrase. It is not only a fun story that makes you *feel* good, but the content of the story can subtly convey to the reader or viewer a desire to *be* good.

Popularity aside, *Harry Potter* has also been criticized in some minor circles for introducing young readers to witchcraft and the occult. However, that criticism would apply to virtually the entire fantasy category of children's literature. Regrettably, Rowling's critics miss the obvious. *Harry Potter* is a fairy tale. To oppose it because of its use of magic is to oppose *Snow White, Peter Pan, Jack and the Beanstalk, The Chronicles of Narnia,* and countless other fairy tales as well. They are all set in secondary worlds where magic is real. Harry, like other fairy-tale characters, is taught to use his gift of wizardry for good.

Although Rowling's story lacks the theological brilliance of Lewis and Tolkien, her *Harry Potter* series is an outstanding morality tale. Consider these seven Christian themes that are introduced in *Harry Potter and the Sorcerer's Stone* and run throughout the entire seven-part series: First, life is a struggle between good and evil. Second, children matter and play a key part in the supernatural realm. That is why evil tries to attack the infant Harry to destroy the hope of the future. Third, every single human being is far more valuable than his limited physical circumstances indicate. Fourth, our gifts should be used for service, not personal power. Fifth, authority and tradition matter—they are powerful sources of wisdom. Sixth, the purpose of education is to develop an individual's gifts and mold moral character. Seventh, and most profoundly Christlike of all, there is no force that can compare to the power of sacrificial love. When Harry does not understand why the evil Professor Quirrell could not bear to be touched by him, Dumbledore explains, "It is because of your mother. She sacrificed herself for you. And that kind of love leaves a mark. No, this kind of mark cannot be seen. It lives in your very skin. Love, Harry. Love."

Although young readers might not be aware of it, the story of Harry's early life is somewhat parallel to the early life of Jesus.

Harry Potter	Jesus
From birth, Harry is the chosen one, destined to defeat the evil Voldemort.	From birth, Jesus is the chosen one, destined to defeat Satan and break the stranglehold of sin that has afflicted humanity.
Voldemort fears that the newborn Harry will someday come to power. In fact, Harry not only survives the murderous attack from Voldemort, but somehow deprives Voldemort of his power in the process.	King Herod feared that the newborn Christ would someday come to power. In truth, in his resurrection Christ became our king in a way that Herod could never have dreamed possible.
Albus Dumbledore, a wise and honorable wizard, recognizes from the beginning the child's special destiny.	Simeon, a man righteous and devout, recognizes from the beginning the child Jesus' messianic destiny.
Harry's relatives, the Dursleys, are disbelievers in magic and reject Harry's special purpose.	Jesus' relatives in Nazareth reject his special purpose, claiming, "He has gone out of his mind" (Mark 3:21).
Voldemort tempts Harry with his ultimate desire—to have his parents alive again.	Satan tempts Jesus with the ultimate human desire—to have dominion over the world.

What fairy tales can proclaim in fantasy, Christianity proclaims in reality. Jesus Christ, the divine king of kings, bestows honor and a share of divinity upon each and every human person. Jesus is a king who bows before us. Jesus is the master who serves his servants. He washed *our* feet. He died so that we might live and rose to reveal our future place in glory. We are special because the most special God loves us.

Whether or not the Christian parallels are fully realized by the reader or viewer is not important. Christ can work, hidden between the lines, on an unconscious level, calling the children to come unto him. It is in this hidden way that the magic of *Harry Potter,* far from being a danger, can be an ally.

Fairy tales last because they convey truths that go beyond any generation's fashions or fads. From the very beginning of her story, Rowling interwove timeless fairy-tale themes into the world of *Harry Potter.* Just as the infant Aurora in *Sleeping Beauty* is hidden away in a cottage in the woods, Harry is given over to the care of his "muggle" relatives, the Dursleys. Harry, like Cinderella, is subjected to the scorn and abuse of his relatives. He lives in a cupboard under the stairs and is treated as a servant rather than as a family member. Through the first ten years of his life, Harry is kept in ignorance of the special circumstances surrounding his birth. Despite this, he does not allow the circumstances to make him bitter. In fact, like Cinderella's nasty stepsisters, it is Dudley, the Dursley's real son, who is the bitter apple that has not fallen far from the family tree. Ironically, it is Dudley who is more abused by his parents than Harry. Dudley suffers from neglect, the neglect of discipline.

All of this changes for Harry with the arrival of a magical letter, delivered by carrier owl, which announces, to Harry's surprise, his acceptance to Hogwarts School of Witchcraft and Wizardry and thus begins his entry into the magical world he has been destined to join. Boarding the Hogwarts Express through a magical barrier on Platform 9¾ at King's Cross Station, Harry embarks on the adventure of a lifetime, filled with an enchanted castle, a mirror that shows one's true desires, dragon eggs, an invisibility cloak, Quiddich matches, and, most overdue for Harry, real friends like Hermione Granger and Ron Weasley. And like Dorothy in Oz, he discovers that all is not well in the world of magic, so Harry must choose to develop his magical powers for good and not evil.

To equip Harry to do battle with the evil wizardry that has haunted his past, he is brought to Hogwarts School, where the approach to education is to prepare students for life, not just to train them for careers. The young wizards-in-training are expected to respect the authority of the teachers and follow the rules. Under the guidance of the headmaster, Albus Dumbledore, Harry is taught to develop his magical powers for good and not for evil. Hogwarts teaches a class entitled "Defense Against the Dark Arts." Hogwarts values tradition, not the latest educational trend. Hogwarts is without computers and smart boards—ink bottles and quills will suffice. Most importantly, Hogwarts does not teach its students how to compromise their principles to get on in the world. It recognizes the existence of a spiritual realm and teaches that there are right and wrong ways to interact with that realm.

In the fairy-tale world, the battle between good and evil is real. It is in this battle that Harry shows his heroism. The young reader who can identify with Harry might also identify with Harry's virtuous choices. Having been subjected to more than his share of tragedy, which would break the moral fiber of many adults, let alone children, Harry stands up against evil. Like a true hero, he saves Hermione's life by battling the troll. He confronts Voldemort, refusing to give in to his demand for the precious Sorcerer's Stone. He does not compromise. When Voldemort tells Harry, "There is no such thing as good or evil; there is only power, and those too weak to seek it," Harry calls him a liar. He fights for his parents' honor, for his friends, and for his newfound Hogwarts home.

There are many Voldemorts in the real world who will confront our children. Voldemort's minions are everywhere, constructing their culture of death. But in Harry's popularity, there is hope. The *Harry Potter* phenomenon can be the start of a "children's crusade" for the twenty-first century. Tired of grown-up executives who have pandered sleaze and cynicism at them from all directions, they have rebelled. And they are joined by millions of adults who claim the right to a childlike life themselves—and who are as eager as the children to read the books and watch the movies. They are not afraid to put their money where their hearts are. "Potterism" is a rebellion against the meaninglessness, cynicism, and selfishness that surround children today. They do not want to see themselves as bratty and narcissistic—the Draco Malfoys of the world. In a world that preaches "pleasure now," "truth is relative," and "look out for yourself," the young-at-heart still hunger for romance and adventure, honor and virtue.

Long live childhood. Long live Harry Potter.

18

Signs

FAITH IS THE ANTIDOTE TO FEAR.

*Blinding Edge Pictures /
Buena Vista Pictures* (2002)

Producer	Frank Marshal
Director	M. Night Shyamalan
Author of Screenplay	M. Night Shyamalan
Running Time	106 minutes

MAIN CHARACTERS

Graham "Father" Hess	Mel Gibson
Merrill Hess	Joaquin Phoenix
Morgan Hess	Rory Culkin
Bo Hess	Abigail Breslin
Colleen Hess	Patricia Kalember
Ray Reddy (veterinarian)	M. Night Shyamalan

Crop circles in fields of corn. Extraterrestrial prophecies from picture books. Unidentified flying objects hovering in the sky. An alien invasion. A planetary Armageddon. Clearly, this is the stuff of science fiction on a global scale.

But *Signs* is not about the world or about science. *Signs* focuses on a solitary man and his family. It is all about faith. Film critic Roger Ebert said it best when he wrote, "Here is a movie in which the plot is the rhythm section, not the melody." The melody is miracle. The composer is God. Can you hear the music? Can you see the signs?

In the tradition of Alfred Hitchcock, Catholic director M. Night Shyamalan, noted for his work in *The Sixth Sense* and *Unbreakable,* cultivates a sense of apprehension in the audience by what he doesn't show. Silence is scary. Darkness is disturbing. Inaction is unsettling. By drawing us into the characters' points of view, we feel what they feel. We identify with their fear because fear of the unknown is one thing we all have in common.

Most of the days of our lives are pretty ordinary. Days stretch into weeks, weeks into months, and months into years. Numbed by the routine and familiar, we get tricked into thinking that we are pretty much in charge, that we are captains of our own ships. And then, *it* happens. Something unexpected. Something horrible. And in an instant, we can't lean on all the people and things that we had gotten used to relying on, especially ourselves. These critical moments reveal the kind of person we really are.

Signs is the story of Graham Hess, a former reverend who is barely holding on to his family. At the film's beginning, we see Graham walking in his hallway. On the wall behind him is the out-line of a cross that had hung there for so long, it had preserved the wallpaper under it from discoloration. The cross is no longer there. Hess has taken it down because he no longer believes in God. A year earlier, a driver asleep at the wheel had killed his beloved wife, while she was out for an evening walk. When she died, his faith died with her. He is alone.

And then—something happens. Something is wrong. Dogs are barking. The wind sounds eerie. There is something or some-one out there in his cornfield. Something hostile. Something dan-gerous. Graham's family is filled with apprehension. They need faith, hope, strength, and spiritual comfort from their Dad. They want the reassurance that we all want. We crave faith and hope like a starving person craves bread and water. In the real story of life, we all long for a happy ending.

But if there is no God, then there is no plan to the universe. The universe has no objective meaning. Therefore, life has no ultimate meaning. There is no rhyme or reason to anything or anyone. The human animal is just the result of blind evolutionary chance. We are an accident of the universe. "Life," as Shakespeare's Macbeth observes, "is a tale told by an idiot, full of sound and fury, signifying nothing."

When God is absent from our culture, the prophets of nihilism take center stage, proclaiming that we must "live for the moment because the moment is all we have. Take pleasure, for pleasure is all there is. Serve yourself, since you are all you've got." As attractive as this message may sound, there is something in it that rings hollow in our ears. The prophets of nihilism peddle empty calories to a malnourished world.

Signs allows us to vicariously identify our fear with the fear that grips the Hess family. If they resolve their fears, perhaps we might resolve our own. And in a moment of quiet conversation between Graham and his brother, Merrill, Graham reveals the way out of fear, a way that he can no longer follow:

> People break down into two groups when they experience something lucky. Group number one sees it as more than luck, more than coincidence. They see it as a sign, the evidence that there is someone out there watching over them. Group number two sees it as just pure luck and a happy turn of chance. [For unbelievers,] deep down, they feel that whatever happens, they are on their own. And that fills them with fear. [For believers,] deep down, they feel that whatever's going to happen, there will be someone there to help them. And that fills them with hope. So what you have to ask yourself is: What kind of person are you? Are you the kind that sees signs, sees miracles, or do you believe that people just get lucky? Or look at the question this way: is it possible that there are no coincidences?

God or no God? That is *the* question. If there is a God, then I can rely on someone greater than myself, greater than the power of death, to give me hope even when death is imminent. If there is a God, then I am never alone, even when I feel most alone. If there is a God, then everything has meaning. Everything is a sign of God's presence, God's care, God's longing for us as we long for God.

Yet, even when faced with the fright of an alien invasion, Graham continues to deny. Grief can be so overwhelming that it can become a barrier that blocks out God. Our pain can be so deafening that we can no longer hear God's voice, our eyes so filled with tears that we can no longer see God's presence. Such is the case with Graham. His daughter Bo asks him, "Why do you talk to Mom when you are by yourself? Does she ever answer back?"

"No," replies Graham.

"She never answers me either." Bo can only compensate for her fears by obsessing over clean water, filling up countless glasses of water that she scatters throughout the house. Graham's son, Morgan, senses his father's isolation as well. Morgan can't rely on his own father, because what he needs from his father is faith. But Graham cannot give what he does not have. In the absence of faith, there is only fear.

On what could be their last night together, with the windows boarded up in expectation of an alien attack, Graham encourages each of his children to pick a favorite meal. He offers them any food they wish—a last supper of French toast, spaghetti, and a cheeseburger with extra bacon. Graham can offer them everything except what they most need—the cup of eternal salvation, which Jesus offered his disciples at his Last Supper. But Graham cannot offer an eternity he cannot see. Initially, they are pleased about having their favorite foods. But before eating, they begin to sense an emptiness still within. They look to their Dad for something more. Morgan insists on a prayer before the meal. "I'm not wasting one more minute of my life on prayer. Not one minute!" Graham declares in anger, only exacerbating the rift between father and son. But prayer is exactly what they need. One can only wonder how many families throughout the world feast on food but starve for lack of prayer.

It was Graham's love for his wife and the anguish he felt over losing her that drove him to deny God, to be all alone, to be filled with fear. Yet it is his love for his family that drives him back to God as well. Finally, in one of the film's most dramatic moments, Graham faces the concrete reality of death, as his son struggles with a life-threatening asthma attack. When there is no other place or person to turn to, not even to himself, Graham turns back to God. Only the Creator can heal his son. God is his only hope.

Graham's love for his son pushes him back to God, a God he has avoided and denied. Finally, at a critical point, he expresses to God the anger that he has suppressed for months and makes contact once again. "Don't do this to me again. Not again. I hate you. I hate you," he declares with tears in his eyes. He acknowledges God once again. He believes. Love brings him back to faith; faith brings him back to life. With conviction in his voice once again, he counsels Morgan through his critical asthma attack:

> Fear is feeding it. Don't be afraid of what's happening. Believe it's going to pass. Just wait. Don't be afraid. The air is coming. Don't be afraid. It's about to pass. Believe. Here comes the air. Feel my chest. Breathe with me. Don't be afraid, Morgan. Feel me breathe. Breathe with me together. The air is going in our lungs. We're the same. We're the same.

As the son returns to the father, so, too, the son returns to his Creator, God. He is one with God, just as his son is one again with him.

Graham's brother, Merrill had been a great baseball hitter in high school, but too many strikeouts had cost him a professional career. "It felt wrong not to swing," Merrill said. Despite his own disappointments, Merrill was quietly supportive of his brother throughout Graham's time of grief and his crisis of faith. But after their night of fright, the usually timid younger brother gives Graham a serious wake-up call for the future. "Listen," Merrill says, "there are some things I can take and a couple things I can't. One of them I can't take is when my older brother who is everything that I want to be starts losing faith in things. I saw that look in your eyes last night. I don't ever want to see your eyes like that again. OK? I'm serious." In so many words, Merrill tells Graham to get his "spiritual act together." A well-needed sermon.

But can faith in God give Graham the power to deliver his family from danger? The spiritual life of his family and the mortal life of his child hang in the balance of his decision. Does he see the signs? Does he believe in a God who loves, who encodes messages through creation?

To save his child, Graham has to believe. He has to believe in signs. If he doesn't, his child dies. It is a matter of life or death. What kind of person does he choose to be? Could Bo's dreams of danger and her quirky obsession with clean water have a deeper meaning? Could Morgan's asthma be not a curse, but a blessing that one day saves him? Could Merrill's love of hitting a baseball have been for a grander purpose? Could Colleen's dying words be a message from a loving God?

Yes or no to God? Faith or fear? Only Graham can answer.

Could all the sufferings and confusions in the world be part of a plan in the hand of God? Does God communicate through our flaws? Could a hidden, loving God be sending us signs? Could our worst pain lead to our greatest joy?

Yes or no to God? Faith or fear? Only we can answer.

Graham chooses God. He obeys what he discerns God to be telling him. He surrenders himself and, in doing so, finds his faith and loses his fear. He finds confidence in God's strength. With a newfound assuredness in his voice, Graham says, "Swing away, Merrill. Swing away." With baseball bat in hand, Merrill does battle with the demonic alien, paralleling the prophecy of Jesus: "And these signs will accompany those who believe: by using my name they will cast out demons" (Mark 16:17).

What kind of God does our Christian faith reveal? It reveals a God who is intensely interested in our everyday walk through life. God loves beyond the conjectures of our wildest imagination. God is found in the details. God brings good from evil.

The film *Signs* is an existentialist argument for faith in God: it challenges us to look within ourselves. Deep in the fiber of our being, we have a fundamental need for God—a longing no drink can quench, no food can satisfy, no human can remedy. As Saint Augustine wrote, "You have made us for yourself. And our hearts are restless until they rest in you."

We were created for happiness. Our destiny lies in choosing to walk the path of faith that God has paved for us. We will not walk it alone. These signs, these glimpses of another world may be fleeting, but they are enough—for us to believe in an invisible reality that guides us through the visible reality. As said earlier, Saint-Exupéry understood this truth when he wrote in *The Little Prince:* "It is only with the heart that one can see rightly, what is essential is invisible to the eye."

If we forget the next world, we become ineffective in this one. If we reject the light of God, this world becomes total darkness—like a ship lost at sea without starlight to guide her. Accept the light and we will see—slowly at first, as our spiritual eyes adjust to the uncreated light of God—but more and more with time. With more wisdom comes more love. With more love comes more joy.

The signs of God's love are all around us. We live in the midst of miracle.

19

The Count of Monte Cristo

SUFFERING CAN BE REDEMPTIVE.

Spyglass Entertainment /
Touchstone Pictures (2002)

Producer	Gary Barber
Director	Kevin Reynolds
Author of Screenplay	Jay Wolpert
Running Time	131 minutes

MAIN CHARACTERS

Edmond Dantes	Jim Caviezel
Fernand Mondego	Guy Pearce
Mercedes	Dagmara Dominczyk
Abbé Faria	Richard Harris
Villefort	James Frain

Scriptwriter Jay Wolpert is faithful to the well-known Alexander Dumas story to a point, but to make a better point, his and director Kevin Reynolds' version of the story goes in a direction Dumas would never have approved—the direction of Christianity. *The Count of Monte Cristo* is a classic story of revenge that is transformed into a story of redemption.

The Count of Monte Cristo is the story of Edmond Dantes, a loyal shipman who is unwittingly tricked by Napoleon into carrying a

169

seditious letter from Corsica to France. For Napoleon, there are only two kinds of people: "Kings and pawns, emperors and fools," he declares, while watching Dantes embark for France. Edmond Dantes had become merely a pawn to be sacrificed to save Napoleon's greater kingship.

Upon his return to his hometown in France, his best friend Fernand Mondego betrays him to Villefort, the local magistrate. Beneath the guise of friendship, Mondego had secretly envied Dantes' goodness as well as his beautiful fiancée, Mercedes. "Yours is a life truly blessed, Edmond," Mondego enviously declares. When Villefort discovers that the letter would implicate him in treason, he immediately condemns the innocent Dantes to a life in exile at the horrid Chateau di'f, a prison whose only release is death.

In an instant, everything and everyone that matter are taken from Dantes—his freedom, job, father, and lover—everything except his God. He falls from ship's captain to prisoner, from betrothed to alone. When the imprisoned Edmond cries out to God in the pain of torture, the sadistic warden sarcastically replies, "God is never in France this time of year." At first, Edmond clings to a message scratched into the wall of his prison cell, *God will give me justice.* But slowly, throughout the years of solitary confinement and torture, Edmond's faith fails. He turns his back on a God who would turn his back on him. Years alone in a cell of stone finally harden Edmond Dantes' heart.

Betrayed by Napoleon, by Villefort, and by Mondego, Edmond Dantes finally felt betrayed by God. Dantes had led a good life, and up until that time, having never encountered the level of evil embodied in Villefort and Mondego, Dantes had believed, like so many of us, that goodness would be rewarded in this life. What Edmond did not realize is that goodness is not always rewarded, but often punished. His nobility leads him to be manipulated by Napoleon, his innocence makes him a victim for Villefort, and his purity only creates scorn in the heart of Mondego. Edmond Dantes was loyal, compassionate, and honest, and for that he was betrayed.

If there is a religion on the planet that should understand this, it's Christianity. Yet, we Christians often miss the message before our eyes. At the heart of our faith stands a symbol that is an executioner's tool—the crucifix. The imagery is clear, yet often the message is lost. Unlike Buddha, who was well praised after his enlightenment, or Mohammed, who was made a ruler, Jesus, God incarnate, was spared no misfortune. In fact, by his very being, Jesus provoked anger and hatred. Like a mirror, he reflected back to us an image of ourselves that we did not want to see. How could Edmond, a good man raised in a Christian world, not have known that goodness can provoke punishment? How can we?

Edmond Dantes' rejection of God is regrettable but understandable considering the degree of torment he faced. Edmond's cross was a cross he could not bear alone. But he was never alone. Particularly, God was with him in the person of the priest, Abbé Faria, a fellow prisoner of the Chateau di'f who even found God in the sunlight he had been deprived of for years. A former military man, the priest had lost God in his life on the outside of prison, but in his penance for crimes done to humanity, he had found God on the inside. His warm heart contrasted starkly with that of Dantes, who had faith in God on the outside but had lost him on the inside of a cold prison.

Unlike the character of Jean Valjean from *Les Misérables,* who found his moral center in the kindness of a priest, Edmond Dantes only seeks power from Abbé Faria—the power to seek vengeance on those who had betrayed him, the power to become what he hates.

Edmond thought he had lost everything, but he had lost more than everything: he had lost God. In the absence of God, something always fills the void—for Dantes, it is vengeance. Edmond idolizes his hate in the absence of loving God.

We become like what we worship. If we worship God, we become more Godlike. If we worship a false idol, we compromise our humanity. Worshiping empty idols leaves us empty, and an empty soul can be filled with hate.

After thirteen years of unjust imprisonment, Edmond Dantes escapes and finds the buried treasure of which Abbé Faria had secretly told him. He is now powerful and free. Or is he? Although Edmond Dantes left the prison, the prison of vengeance never left him. On some level, he understands this when he declares, "Goodbye, priest. You are free now, as I never will be." Hatred makes us identify more with our enemy than with those we love. Vengeance is a bonding more to the perpetrator of evil than to the victim. Seeking vengeance on those who had wounded him, he becomes a shadow of what he once was. To slay a dragon, Edmond becomes a dragon. Edmond Dantes, a lamb led to the slaughter, becomes the count of Monte Cristo, a wolf in the fold.

Dantes' choice is all too human. Revenge is a natural response to being wronged. Fair enough. But have we not been given supernatural gifts of grace to help us transcend our sinful inclinations? Doesn't Christ call us to justice and mercy rather than to vengeance? When we seek vengeance, we become what we hate. But when we seek justice, we protect what we love. When we seek love, we become what we were meant to be.

The Christian call to love is not a call to passivity in the face of evil. Love includes justice; it does not deny it. Righteous anger is justifiable, even necessary. It is not a sin to cry out against inhumanity. Christ drove the moneychangers out of the Temple. He was the perfect Son defending his Father's house.

It is important to distinguish between vengeance and justice. Vengeance wills harm, not restitution. Justice is giving each person the rights that are due him or her. Revenge takes pleasure in another person's pain. Justice takes comfort in defending another person *from* pain.

In Dumas' book, when Edmond completes the plot of revenge, he sails away. But in reality, revenge does not end so neatly, because each act of vengeance is the beginning of new potential chain reactions of hate. For every act of vengeance, there is an equal and opposite act of vengeance. The chain reaction does not end until the chain is broken. It cannot be broken without personal sacrifice. Love, again, is the answer. It takes something supernatural to break a natural chain of vengeance. Someone must bear the pain without willing to inflict it on others.

Disguised as the count of Monte Cristo, Dantes weaves himself back into the lives of his betrayers to sow the seeds of revenge.

Mondego had taken Mercedes as his wife after telling her that Edmond was dead, and they have a son as old as Edmond's years in prison. Attending a birthday party given in honor of Mondego's son, the count offers this toast:

> Life is a storm, my friend. You will bask in the sunlight one moment and be shattered on the rocks the next. What makes you a man is what you do when that storm comes. You must look into that storm and shout as you did in Rome. "Do your worst. For I will do mine." Then the fates will know you as we know you: as Albert Mondego, the man.

The count of Monte Cristo's toast was close to the truth, but tragically flawed. When the storms of suffering come our way, we must shout out the opposite of the count's words. When evil does its worst, we must do our *best*.

Given the opportunity to reach out to his beloved Mercedes, the count spurns her, "If you ever loved me, don't rob me of my hate. It's all I have left—Edmond Dantes is dead." The count of Monte Cristo is so intent on destroying the two men he hates that he cannot reach out to the one woman he loves. Revenge is not sweet or even sour. It is poisonous.

Equally trapped in his choices is the character of Fernand Mondego—a Judas Iscariot with a scabbard—who never finds any happiness in his betrayal. "I couldn't live in a world where you have everything and I have nothing," he says to Dantes. Mondego may have everything, but that is of no benefit to a man who is nothing. Evil is its own punishment. Even in deceiving and marrying Mercedes, she can only be another worthless possession gathering dust in the tomb that is his house but never a home. The joyless cannot bring joy either to others or to themselves.

As Christians, we should not be surprised by the dead rising; it is the core of our faith. Despite the horrendous circumstances of Dantes' imprisonment, he had known companionship with Abbé Faria and love from Mercedes. God had not abandoned Edmond

Dantes. In the film's dramatic conclusion, realizing the love he has for Mercedes and discovering that he is the father of her son, Dantes lets Mondego go free. Love transforms him. He stops the cycle of vengeance. Whereas critics might dismiss Dantes' turnabout as simply a convenient "happy ending" against a book that offers none, Christians cannot be so dismissive. If the cycle is ever to end, it must end by someone bearing the burden of innocent suffering and responding in love, as Christ did for us. Love transforms us.

But is the Christian interpretation of *The Count of Monte Cristo* wishful thinking, or is it a true subtext of the story? Who better to ask than the man who played Edmond Dantes?

As fortune would have it, I was given the opportunity to meet Catholic actor Jim Caviezel, and we discussed his thoughts on the film. Fairly shy and quiet in demeanor, particularly when referring to himself, Jim's eyes lit up and his voice became impassioned when he began speaking of God. For him, God played an integral part in the film story of *The Count of Monte Cristo,* just as he plays an integral part in the life of Jim Caviezel. For Jim, matters of God are matters of the heart.

I asked the actor about the count's transformation at the story's dramatic ending, when Dantes gives up seeking vengeance, yet still fights for justice in the final climactic swordfight with Mondego. Caviezel likened it to a soldier at war who fights to protect the family behind him. Dantes' final swordfight is not done out of hate for Mondego but out of love for Mercedes and his son. Caviezel sees the whole film-story as one of "redemptive suffering."

With intensity growing in his voice, Jim Caviezel noted how God remained present in the life of Edmond Dantes, even in the prison at Chateau di'f. "God had a grip on Edmond's heart through the character of the priest," Caviezel explained, "even though Edmond only wanted from the priest to learn how to kill. Despite this, God began working on Edmond." Citing the lines by heart, Caviezel smiled as he recited Abbé Faria's dying words to Edmond Dantes:

"Here is your final lesson: do not commit the crime for which you now serve the sentence. God said, 'Vengeance is mine.'"

"I don't believe in God."

"That doesn't matter. He believes in you."

"God's hold on us" is a powerful subtext in the film as it is in the life of actor Jim Caviezel.

It is fitting that Edmond gives the chess piece of a king to Mondego in their final confrontation. "King's to you, Fernand." It was Mondego who had tried to live like a king, treating others like his subjects, yet his soul remained a pawn to the whims of sin. Edmond ultimately rejects the kingship of superiority. The count of Monte Cristo is renounced in order for Edmond Dantes to live again.

In the end, Dantes realizes that Abbé Faria's wisdom was the treasure buried beneath the treasure at Monte Cristo. It is the wisdom of the ages, the wisdom of Christ.

In the film's epilogue, Dantes stands truly free with his wife and child on the cliffs of the Chateau di'f and speaks to the heavens the wisdom he now shares with his priest friend, a wisdom born of repentance. "You were right priest. You were right. All that was used for vengeance will be used for good. So rest in peace my friend." Dantes has found peace as well. In the end, he is neither a king nor a pawn, but a man, having chosen redemption over revenge.

20

The Lord of the Rings

ONE CROSS TO SERVE THEM ALL.
New Line Cinema (2001–2003)

Director and Main Producer	Peter Jackson
Authors of Screenplays	Fran Walsh/Philippa Boyens/ Peter Jackson
Running Times	approx. 200 minutes

MAIN CHARACTERS

Frodo Baggins	Elijah Wood
Samwise Gamgee	Sean Astin
Gandalf	Ian McKellen
Aragorn	Viggo Mortensen
Gimli	John Rhys-Davies
Legolas	Orlando Bloom
Arwen	Liv Tyler
Eowyn	Miranda Otto
Saruman	Christopher Lee

While marking test papers one day at Oxford University, J. R. R. Tolkien, professor of philology, began to daydream. "In a hole in the ground there lived a hobbit," he wrote. Like a magician conjuring up a potion, Tolkien began to construct one of the most imaginative and well-thought-out mythological stories ever published.

Millions have been captured by its spell, first with *The Hobbit,* and then with its more serious and successful sequel, *The Lord of the Rings,* which is not a typical Disneylike fantasy. When we enter Middle-earth, we find a world dominated by elves, not by humans. Borrowing from northern mythology and Anglo-Saxon legends, Tolkien's elves are poetic and noble beings who stand about six feet tall. Dwarves are skilled craftsmen and fierce fighters who have constructed spectacular cities underneath the ground. And in addition to wizards and humans, Tolkien added a simple, peace-loving people known as hobbits and placed them at the heart of his adventure.

Fans of Tolkien's classic, which was voted in England as the most important book of the twentieth century, waited with much anticipation for director Peter Jackson's movie version of *The Lord of the Rings.* Jackson filmed the entire ten-plus-hour saga in one production and released the film in three installments. *Part One: The Fellowship of the Ring* premiered in December 2001, with *Part Two: The Two Towers* and *Part Three: The Return of the King* coming out in subsequent years. Together, these three comprise a film interpretation (never the same as the book) of one epic story—a story that centers on something so simple and small that its appearance might deceive us into thinking that it is harmless. But it is not; it is deadly. And upon its destruction hangs the survival of Middle-earth.

The Fellowship of the Ring begins with the origin of the ring. An evil demon named Sauron fashioned the ring to control all the other magic rings of Middle-earth, infusing it with much of his own power so that he might rule the world. As the elvin Queen Galadriel explains, "And into this ring he poured his cruelty, his malice and his will to dominate all life. One ring to rule them all." But during a magnificent battle, when Sauron was on the verge of subjugating all the creatures of Middle-earth, the ring was cut off his finger and lost, only to be found centuries later by a hobbit named Bilbo Baggins. Bilbo had found the ring in a cave, taking it from its former possessor, Gollum, who had been cursed by the ring for five hundred years. Now, Sauron, the lord of the rings, and his minions are again on the rise, and he must get back his evil possession. If successful, all the creatures of

Middle-earth—elves, dwarves, humans, and hobbits—will be under his darkness. Sent by angelic powers to fight Sauron, Gandalf the wizard arrives in the Shire, the hobbit's idyllic country village, to set in motion a desperate quest to destroy the ring. Gandalf explains what is at stake:

> Sauron needs only this ring to cover all the lands with a second darkness. He is seeking it, seeking it, all his thought is bent on it. The ring yearns to go home, to return to the hand of its master. They are one, the ring and the dark lord. Frodo, he must never find it.

Bilbo's younger nephew, Frodo, must carry the evil ring to Sauron's own land of Mordor, and destroy the ring by throwing it into the fires that first forged it on Mount Doom.

At the heart of *The Lord of the Rings* lies a fundamental moral and spiritual dilemma: *How do we undo an evil that never should have been?* Tolkien knows the answer. There is only one way, and the answer is found within *The Lord of the Rings.*

It should not surprise us that Tolkien would use a ring as a symbol of evil. The line of the circular ring is sealed in upon itself and incapable of growing. As English author G. K. Chesterton said in his book *Orthodoxy*, "For the circle is perfect and infinite in its nature; but it is fixed forever in its size; it can never be larger or smaller." But the circle does not define the true human condition. Through the character of Aragorn, Tolkien proclaims, "Behold! We are not bound forever to the circles of the world, and beyond them is more than memory." In contrast, it is the shape of the cross that better symbolizes the truth of reality. Again quoting Chesterton from *Orthodoxy*, "But the cross, though it has at its heart a collision and a contradiction, can extend its four arms forever without altering its shape. Because it has a paradox in its center it can grow without changing."[12] Symbolically, the cross is the antithesis of the circle. Similarly, in *The Lord of the Rings*, the mystery of the cross, hidden within the story, provides the antidote that will counter the power of the ring.

I have met many enthusiastic fans of *The Lord of the Rings* over the years. Some have extensive knowledge about Middle-earth through Tolkien's other work, *The Silmarillion*. Still others can even speak elvish, one of the seventeen languages Tolkien invented for Middle-earth. Yet, these same people are surprised when I mention that there are powerful *Christian* themes running throughout all of *The Lord of the Rings*.

How could they miss the theological messages? The answer lies in Tolkien's understanding of how a story can impact the reader's imagination. He does not try to hit the reader over the head with the Christian faith. Few of the characters speak about their religious beliefs or engage in acts of religious devotion. Rather, the Christian elements are subtly woven into the very fabric of the story, so that those who might be disposed to reject religious truths would encounter them on a deeper level. In a letter he wrote to Robert Murray, SJ (Letter 156), Tolkien wrote:

> I have purposely kept all [religious] allusions to the highest matters down to mere hints, perceptible only by the most attentive, or kept them under unexplained symbolic forms. So God and the "angelic" gods, the Lords or Powers of the West, only peep through in such places as Gandalf's conversation with Frodo. [13]

A fellow Oxford writer, Stratford Caldecott, described it this way: "*The Lord of the Rings* is not a book *about* religion, but it is the expression of a religious soul working under God."

In a letter to a friend, Tolkien himself described *The Lord of the Rings* as "a fundamentally religious work; unconsciously so at first, but consciously in the revision." Tolkien went on to explain, "That is why I have not put in, or have cut out, practically all references to anything like 'religion,' to cults or practices, in the imaginary world. For the religious element is absorbed into the story and the symbolism." *The Lord of the Rings* is about living faith, not speaking about it. It is an attempt to involve the reader in the realm of God without them knowing it. Tolkien placed God under the radar, so his presence could not be obviously detected. Operating on an unconscious level, it can have a more powerful influence. Christian themes run *through* the story, but are not overtly mentioned *in* the story. The God of Christianity may be unseen, but is at the very heart of the narrative. The unnamed God not only inspired the story, but he plays an absolutely vital role in it as well.

The Christian themes in *The Lord of the Rings* are as abundant as the wine Jesus made from water at the wedding feast in Cana. There is so much truth to taste; I can only offer a mere sample. Think of these themes as seven jars of clay, filled to the brim with theological wine, and served to the viewer throughout the story.

The First Jar of Wine—The Nature of Evil

We live in a fallen world, where evil is a clear and present danger. Because of sin, the world has become what C. S. Lewis described as "enemy-occupied territory." The evil that we encounter emanates from a source far more powerful than humanity, but not remotely equal to God. Evil is real and its presence in the world precedes human desire. We see this in *The Lord of the Rings* in the demon Sauron, who parallels the story of Satan. Made as a valar (angel), Sauron was not given one or two attributes of Illuvatar's (God's) personality, but was given a little of every part. Because of this, he proudly saw himself as equal to Illuvatar. In actuality, he played God—the sin of pride. Sauron is not evil because he desires to destroy; he is evil because he desires to create. Creating, in the strict sense of the word, is the sole dominion of God. In usurping God's rightful place, Sauron can only deform and distort what is already created.

Thus, evil is a parasite that has no reality of its own. The destruction it causes, however, is very real. Evil destroys what was originally created as good. Like a black hole, it devours all created things around it. Like an eternal fire, evil exists only to consume other things. Through the corruption of evil, elves have become orcs, ents have become trolls, and nine men have become wraiths, shadows of what they once were. Explaining the ringwraiths to Frodo, Aragorn laments, "They were once men—great kings of men. Then Sauron the deceiver gave to them nine rings of power. Blinded by their greed, they took them without question. One by one they've fallen into darkness. Now they are slaves to his will. They are the nazgul, ringwraiths, neither living nor dead." In describing the ringwraiths, Tolkien has given us an image of hell—a shadow dwelling, ultimate nothingness, a state of profound loss.

What Tolkien wrote in fiction, Saint Paul wrote in the form of a letter to the early Christians in Ephesus. Paul elevated their moral struggle to a higher spiritual plane:

> For our struggle is not against enemies of blood and flesh, but against the rulers, against the authorities, against the cosmic powers of this present darkness, against the spiritual forces of evil in the heavenly places. Therefore take up the whole armor of God, so that you may be able to withstand on that evil day, and having done everything, to stand firm.... With all of these, take the shield of faith, with which you will be able to quench all the flaming arrows of the evil one. Take the helmet of salvation, and the sword of the Spirit, which is the word of God. (Eph 6:12–13, 16–17)

The only way to defeat evil is to reject it and choose good. Galadriel refuses the ring despite the fact that if it is destroyed, her ring loses its power to protect Lothlorien. Aragorn refuses the ring, even though he could use it to regain his kingship of Gondor. When Frodo proposes that Gandalf be the one to take the ring to Mount Doom, Gandalf declares, "Don't tempt me, Frodo. I dare not take it, not even to keep it safe. Understand, Frodo, I would use this ring from a desire to do good. But through me, it would wield a power too great and terrible to imagine." To use evil in the battle against evil is to be enslaved by it. Boromir, on the other hand, wishes to use the power of the ring against the dark lord of the rings. Tragically, he doesn't respect the power of evil held within such a tiny ring. "It is a strange fate that we should suffer so much fear and doubt over so small a thing. Such a little thing." His lack of respect for evil's power leads to his downfall.

The heroes of the fellowship choose good even when it appears that the triumph of evil is inevitable. Aragorn buries Boromir even though he knows that the orcs have captured two hobbits, because the right thing to do is to bury the dead honorably. In the words of Gandalf, "All we have to decide is what to do with the time that is given us."

The Second Jar of Wine—Exalted Humility

At the center of the quest to save the world, Tolkien places a most unlikely hero, yet one most like us—Frodo, who is small and reluctant to accept the burden of the ring, but succumbs to the temptation to wear it. Aragorn, on the other hand, is the classic storybook hero, a natural leader who is not afraid to fight. Aragorn is a great man, but Frodo becomes great. Frodo discovers nobility within himself through his trials. Aragorn understands that all is lost unless the ring is destroyed. We admire Aragorn, but we are more like Frodo. At times, we, too, are overcome by the power of evil, overcome by the demands life makes on us. Tolkien is teaching us that the greatest human quality is not strength of will, but rather humility that engenders compassion toward others. In humility, God can work through us, as happens in the lives of Frodo and Sam. As Galadriel reminds the fellowship, "Even the smallest person can change the course of the future." In the end, all of Middle-earth is saved, not by the greatness of a human, but through the humbleness of a hobbit.

The essence of Christianity is an act of humility, surrendering personal power to be remade by the risen Christ. Gandhi was once asked, "If you were given the power to remake the world, what would you do first?" He replied, "I would pray for the power to renounce that power." In the paradoxical world of faith, humility is exalted.

The Third Jar of Wine—Fellowship

The ring holds an evil so great that no person can resist its power. Frodo bears its weight, but he cannot do it alone. At the time of the crisis, men, dwarves, and elves distrusted each other and didn't like one another. Despite their natural animosity, particularly between dwarves and elves, they put their problems aside to face a far greater crisis. If they are not successful, it will spell certain doom for all of Middle-earth. The fate of the world rests on the strength of the fellowship—Frodo, Sam, Merry, Pippin, Gimli, Legolas, Aragorn, Boromir, and Gandalf—nine individuals in contrast to the nine ringwraiths. Galadriel counsels this fragile group, "The quest stands upon the edge of a knife. Stray but a little, and it will fail, to the ruin of all. Yet hope remains while the company is true."

The strength of the fellowship is supported by the strength of individual friendships. Gimli and Legolas' friendship sustains them throughout the quest. Sam's heroic service to Frodo is absolutely critical for the success of the quest. Ironically, Tolkien once declared that he would have not completed *The Lord of the Rings* were it not for his friendship with C. S. Lewis, who critiqued and encouraged his writing from the beginning.

The Lord of the Rings ends triumphantly, but it takes the whole of the fellowship to defeat the ring and Sauron. There are many heroes within the fellowship. Without Frodo's mercy toward Gollum, Gollum would never have been there to take the ring. Without Sam's courageous friendship, carrying the burden of the ring on his back by carrying Frodo, Frodo would never have made it to the Crack of Doom. Without Merry and Pippin alerting the ents, Saruman's minions might have captured Frodo and Sam. Without Gandalf's self-sacrifice in defeating the balrog, the fellowship would have never made it to Mordor. Without Aragorn, Legolas, and Gimli's heroic battles, the ringwraiths or orcs might have killed Frodo and returned the ring to Sauron. Goodness can triumph when we are united against evil with a common vision of how to defeat evil and an attitude of love toward one another.

The Fourth Jar of Wine—Feminine Grace

In a story that is dominated by male characters, there is an important role given to Galadriel, the elvin queen of Lothlorien. She is an "unstained" vision of beauty and grace, to whom Gimli is particularly devoted. It is his respect for her that allows him to see the good within the elves, which deepens his dedication to the fellowship. Tolkien wrote in a letter, "I think it's true that I owe much of this character [Galadriel] to Christian and Catholic teaching and imagination about Mary." Both allow a sword to pierce their heart: Mary must see her beloved Son crucified, while Galadriel must forsake the evil ring and allow Lothlorien no longer to have her protection.

Feminine beauty beneath the skin is also depicted in the character of Eowyn, who does not fear death, only dishonor. When Aragorn asks her what she fears, Eowyn replies, "A cage. To stay behind bars until use and old age accept them and all chance of valor has gone beyond recall or desire." Feminine grace supports the male heroes of Middle-earth, as it has supported men since civilization began.

The Fifth Jar of Wine—Self-Sacrificial Love

There is only one spiritual road that the fellowship must walk down in order to defeat an evil of awful magnitude. It is the same road that Christ walked. Each person must walk to his Mount Doom. The road is self-sacrificial love. Frodo carrying his terrible burden is akin to Christ carrying the cross. Just as Christ carried his cross up Calvary, bearing the weight of the world, Frodo carries his up Mount Doom.

The Shire is eventually saved, but not for Frodo. In the course of his quest, Frodo is wounded by the poison sword of a ringwraith, by Shelob, and mostly by the psychic wounds left by the ring. The ring exacts a spiritual toll on Frodo, who must go to the western realm in order to heal, as does Bilbo. All heroes bear the scars of their loving service.

For every scar, there is also insight gained. In his woundedness, Frodo is able to identify with what Gollum had suffered under the spiritual weight of the ring for five hundred years. There is goodness even in the worst of creatures. "You were not so different from a hobbit once," he says to Gollum. Ever mindful of protecting Frodo, Sam does not calculate the worth of a wretch like Gollum. But Frodo moves beyond justice to mercy. "I have to believe he can come back, Sam," Frodo says. Bearing the ring has made him identify with Gollum's pain. Hope for Gollum is akin to hope for himself.

Frodo's attitude of humility makes him best suited for the quest. His loving self-sacrifice leads him to mercy. Although he could not know it at the time, Frodo's act of mercy for Gollum is critical to the success of the quest. Gandalf had sensed this from the beginning: "My heart tells me that Gollum has some part to play yet, for good or ill before this is over. The pity of Bilbo may rule the fate of many." In *The Two Towers,* there is a scene where Frodo calls Gollum by his old name, Smeagol. For a moment, because of Frodo's compassion, we see past Gollum's grotesque form and see a hint of his hidden dignity.

Love brings us back to life.

The Sixth Jar of Wine—Resurrection

Christ is with the heroes of the fellowship, whether they know his name or not. Gandalf illustrates the presence of Christ in the resurrection moments that follow death-to-self. Even though he is the *best* hope for leading the fight against Sauron, he willingly sacrifices himself to defeat the balrog. At that moment, he gives up any hope of personal triumph. Yet, God uses Gandalf's sacrifice to raise him up even more powerfully—Gandalf the grey becomes Gandalf the white. Through Gandalf's personal sacrifice, God takes the plans of the valar and enlarges them in a way the valar themselves could never have done. As Tolkien explained, "[Gandalf] was sent [to Middle-earth] by a mere prudent plan of the angelic Valar or governors; but Authority [God] had taken up this plan and enlarged it, at the moment of its failure."

The reality of resurrection is glimpsed in human (or hobbit) experience. Frodo voluntarily sacrifices himself, and the world is saved. Aragorn holds on to hope even when the odds are against him, particularly at the battle of Helms Deep, where he accepts the likelihood of his own death, and eventually ascends to the throne of Gondor.

With our faith in the reality of resurrection, death need no longer be seen as the worst of things. Death is not a punishment for humanity, but a release from this fallen world. The elves, on the other hand, being immortal, are doomed to deathlessness. They are cursed to see all the beauty of the world fade away. The time of elves is ending; the age of man is beginning. The elves lack any concrete notion of heaven, because in the history of Middle-earth God had not incarnated himself to reveal heaven as God's kingdom. They originally created their rings as a way to preserve what they ultimately cannot hold on to. But in doing so, they made a technology that can be manipulated by evil, particularly by Sauron. Their motive was good, but the action was wrong. We can't hold on to the things of this fallen world. The permanence the elves seek can only be found in eternity, not in earthly immortality. Resurrection is the door from here to eternity.

In the defeat of Sauron, in the stillness of the Shire, in the beauty of Lothlorien, there are hints of a glorious paradise yet to come. These hints of heaven's glory are in this world, but are not contained by this world. Middle-earth is not their home, only a temporary lodging. It is in these glimpses of glory that heroes find hope.

But in the absence of faith, there can be only fear. Sauron and his minions have forsaken the architect of hope; therefore, in their desperation, they desire a power that would defeat death. This illusory power is what we call magic, and modern magic is exemplified by the machine. In his youth, Tolkien had spent a few years living in the country. He loved nature, particularly trees. Then, circumstances forced him to live in the city, where smokestacks pouring out industrial pollution surrounded him. In this contrast between tree and tower, Tolkien developed a metaphor for good and evil for *The Lord of the Rings.* Sauron's forces have no respect for nature because they have no respect for her Creator. As the evil wizard Saruman declares, "Together, my lord Sauron, we shall rule this Middle-earth. The old world will burn in the fires of industry. Forests will fall. A new order will rise. We will drive the machine of war with the sword and the spear and the iron fist of the orc." Industry without regard for nature is Tolkien's metaphor for a world in rebellion from God. Evil can only clutch at material power, in a desperate attempt to defeat death, an undefeatable foe. In a world too enamored by the machine, we risk seeing ourselves as machines, instead of children of God given the promise of resurrection.

The Seventh Jar of Wine—Providence: The Hand of God

In imitation of Jesus, I have saved the best wine for last—one served throughout the entire feast of *The Lord of the Rings,* but perhaps best appreciated at the quest's dramatic conclusion. Here, we finally reach the answer to our ultimate question: *how do we undo an evil that never should have been?* Tolkien's answer is: *we can't on our own, but God can!* God is not only the inspiration to Tolkien's classic work; God is also a hidden character within *The Lord of the Rings.*

"Humans and hobbits may not know Illuvatar, God of Middle-earth; but in Tolkien's view, Middle-earth is very much his,"[14] wrote David Colbert, author of a study of the mythological elements within *The Lord of the Rings.* Behind the ebb and flow of the entire quest is the unseen hand of God. Tolkien's belief in providence—a divine plan behind all things that happen—illuminates the entire story and resolves the quest. There are no coincidences. God works through human choices. Even evil choices are incorporated into the workings of God and transformed to bring about good, just as the resurrection transformed the cross from an executioner's tool into a symbol of glory. As Fulton Sheen noted, "God can draw *good* out of evil because, while the power of doing evil deeds is ours, the effects of our evil are outside our control, and, therefore, in the hands of God."[15] God draws straight with crooked "lives."

From the quest's beginning, Gandalf subtly noted the hand of God in accepting Frodo as the ring-bearer: "There are other forces at work in this world, Frodo, besides the will of evil. Bilbo was meant to find the ring, in which case you also were meant to have it. And that is an encouraging thought."

The providential hand of God is never more evident than in the way Tolkien concludes the quest to destroy the ring. God works through the good and bad choices made by Frodo, Sam, and Gollum to bring about the triumph of goodness, and the defeat of the lord of the rings.

We identify with Frodo throughout his quest. We have seen him struggle and grow throughout the experience. We see Sam carry the burden of his friend. Finally, nearing his moment of triumph, we hope Frodo will succeed, just as we hope that we will succeed in our life's quest. But he fails. Frodo refuses to give up the ring at the Crack of Doom. As Tolkien explained, "One must face the fact: the power of Evil in the world is *not* finally resistible by incarnate creatures, however good." Frodo endured a supernatural evil in the ring that was more powerful than any mortal creature. No one person has the power to cast the ring into the Crack of Doom. Frodo's failure is a failure of the will. But Gollum's mania for the ring leads him to attack Frodo and take it, and as Gollum rejoices at finally possessing the prized ring, he accidentally falls into the fires of Mount Doom, which consume him and the ring. Gollum ends up doing what he doesn't mean to do. The quest is completed, the world is saved, but not in a way we might have predicted.

Tolkien alters the anticipated ending to the heroic epic. His message to us is more important than our disappointment over Frodo failing. Tolkien didn't want *The Lord of the Rings* to be about the triumph of the will, but rather about the power of humility to engender mercy, and through that mercy and love, divine providence triumphs.

We cannot save ourselves. Only God can. But God wills us to play a vital role in incarnating the divine goodness and love in human history. God works through the free choices we make. Had Frodo lost sympathy for Gollum, or Sam weakened in his friendship with Frodo, all would have been lost. Every human choice for good is a puzzle piece that fits into the larger picture of human salvation that God is constructing. Behind the lord of the rings is the Lord. He is ultimately the Savior of Middle-earth. He chose Frodo and inspired him to carry out the quest. He ennobled Sam's friendship. He held together the fellowship of the ring.

But without Frodo, Aragorn, and Sam freely choosing to fight the good fight, the will of God in this particular situation could not have been accomplished. They are not mere pawns, fated to be moved by the divine player to protect his kingship. They are more like musicians who choose or do not choose to play their individual part in a musical symphony that God conducts and arranges. Like a cellist, flutist, or percussionist, each has a different part to play. Each must surrender their talent to the musical score that is before them if the symphony is to come to life. This sacrifice creates a whole musical sound that is greater than the sum of its parts. Individuals must surrender to the score in order to transform random, individualistic noise into music. If they choose not to play their part, the symphony remains unfinished, and the full effect of the music we need so desperately to hear is lost.

David Mills, senior editor of *Touchstone Magazine,* summarizes the triumph of *The Lord of the Rings* perfectly: "Because Bilbo and Gandalf and the Elves and Frodo and Sam and Faramir all show Gollum mercy and pity, he does what no one could have done on his own, and what he does not intend to do. He casts the Ring into the Crack of Doom and saves the world."[16] God, working through Gollum's moment of personal weakness, enables the fellowship's success.

The Lord of the Rings has resonated so strongly in the hearts of its fans because the story communicates powerful truths, only some of which have been sampled in these seven jars of sacred wine.

Like Middle-earth's fellowship, our Christian fellowship is predicated on goodness, humility, friendship, grace, and sacrificial love. Jesus Christ has achieved victory on our behalf. The war is won. Christianity is our shield, the cross is our sword, and Christ is our Lord. One cross to serve them all.

After-the-Movie
Discussion Questions

Practical Suggestions

For those of you who might be able to use these film studies as a teaching tool, here are a few suggestions:

1. This book is suitable for both adult or youth study groups, or with high school theology classes.
2. Each of the twenty films can easily be rented or purchased for your viewing (Blockbuster, Hollywood Video, and Best Buy).
3. Given the morally objectionable words or scenes in some of our films, Web sites on the Internet, such as Clean Films, sell "cleaned up" versions of films on DVD, minus objectionable scenes and vulgar language, much like movies broadcast on network television. This would be vitally necessary for the classroom viewing of films such as *The Shawshank Redemption*.
4. Some of the films can be grouped artistically, as in the category of fantasy (such as *The Lord of the Rings* and *Star Wars*) or sports (such as *Rudy* and *Hoosiers*). They can also be grouped according to theme.
5. Use the "After-the-Movie Discussion Questions" as a springboard for discussion.

1. Star Wars Episode IV

1. What traditional belief about reality does *Star Wars* uphold?
2. How does Luke exemplify the religious person?
3. How is the character of Han Solo transformed?
4. What is our fundamental choice regarding good and evil?

2. Superman

1. How does myth relate to the gospel?
2. How does the mythology of *Superman* move our imaginations toward the good news of Jesus Christ?
3. How is the story of Jesus the perfect hero story come true?
4. Are there additional parallels to be drawn between the story of Superman and Jesus?
5. Can you think of any other stories that parallel that story of Jesus in the gospel?

3. Amadeus

1. Why was Salieri so hate-filled toward Amadeus?
2. Is salvation a gift or a reward?
3. What was Salieri's tragic flaw?
4. What is the "scandal of grace"?

4. Hoosiers

1. How is basketball analogous to Christianity?
2. Why do some people want to follow Jesus "on their own"?
3. Why is the communal aspect of Christianity so vital?
4. What are the principles taught by Norman Dale that led his team to success?

5. Rain Man

1. What makes the character of Charlie Babbitt so abrasive?
2. What additional problems arise in a relationship with a mentally challenged person?
3. How is Raymond able to bring about a change in Charlie when other people hadn't been able to do so?

4. What spiritual benefits might arise from a "slower-paced" lifestyle?

6. Indiana Jones and the Last Crusade

1. Why is the "leap of faith" essential to following Jesus?
2. Why can't we judge God for the existence of suffering in the world?
3. What was Professor Jones's illumination?

7. Field of Dreams

1. What decision does Ray make that allows for the possibility of his deeper dreams coming true?
2. How is each of the main characters—Ray, his father, Shoeless Joe, Terrance, and Doc Graham—healed by following "the voice"?
3. What kind of God is revealed in *Field of Dreams*?

8. Beauty and the Beast

1. In what ways does our media culture convey a false notion of beauty?
2. What makes Belle able to save the beast?
3. Is the enchanted spell laid upon the beast a curse or a blessing?
4. Are fairy tales for children or adults?

9. Jurassic Park

1. How is *Jurassic Park* a morality play?
2. Why don't the three invited scientists share John Hammond's enthusiasm? How would John Hammond and Dr. Grant represent contrasting approaches to science?
3. What danger is inherent in the "science for the sake of science" mentality?

10. Rudy

1. How is Rudy's pursuit of his dream not selfish?
2. What virtue does Rudy best exhibit?
3. How is Rudy's accomplishment a triumph of grace and not only one of personal motivation?

11. Groundhog Day

1. How does *Groundhog Day* go beyond being a mere romantic comedy?
2. What consequence does Phil experience when he lives life primarily for personal pleasure?
3. How does *Groundhog Day* demonstrate the relationship between happiness and goodness?

12. The Shawshank Redemption

1. In your judgment, when bad things happen to good people, what should good people do?
2. How does the metaphor of prison relate to the human condition?
3. What characteristic does Andy possess that enables him to survive and thrive as a human being?

13. Forrest Gump

1. How is Forrest heroic?
2. Which is more important: intelligence or wisdom? How is this illustrated in *Forrest Gump*?
3. Were the Beatles right when they sang the words, "All you need is love"? Explain why or why not.

14. Life Is Beautiful

1. How does *Life Is Beautiful* differ from the typical romantic comedy?
2. What attitude choice enables Guido to believe that "life is beautiful"?
3. Why does Guido create the "game" for Joshua in the camp?

15. The Truman Show

1. How should we interpret the scriptural command to "be not conformed to this world"?
2. What is Truman able to do that makes him a "true-man," a true person?
3. Why is Sylvia so important to Truman's final decision to leave Seahaven?
4. In addition to Christof and the actors on the Seahaven set, are the viewers who watch the televised *Truman Show* also complicit in the evil deception being targeted at Truman?

16. Les Misérables

1. How did Valjean find redemption after years in prison?
2. How is Christ's new law radically different from the old law that Javert followed?
3. How does law relate to love?
4. Contrast Saint Paul with Javert.

17. Harry Potter and thd Sorcerer's Stone

1. What is it about the Harry Potter series that has made it so popular with young readers?
2. How does the film affirm the value of children?
3. How does Harry's childhood parallel the childhood story of Jesus?
4. Are there additional fairy-tale images in the Harry Potter story?

18. Signs

1. How is *Signs* more a movie about God than a movie about aliens?
2. What is the fundamental choice each human being must make? How does it affect his or her outlook on life?
3. How does Graham's relationship with his son, Morgan, parallel God's relationship with us?

19. The Count of Monte Cristo

1. How is the ending of the 2002 film version of this story radically different from that in the classic book? Is the ending satisfying?
2. Why can goodness provoke the response of hatred and even violence from others?
3. Why isn't revenge ultimately satisfying?

20. The Lord of the Rings

1. How is *The Lord of the Rings* fundamentally a religious story?
2. Why wasn't Boromir correct? Can evil ever be used to fight evil?
3. Why is the notion of a "fellowship" so critical to Tolkien's idea of fighting spiritual evil?

Notes

1. C. S. Lewis, *Surprised by Joy* (New York: Harcourt, Brace, Jovanovich Publishers, 1984), 236.

2. C. S. Lewis, *The Collected Letters of C. S. Lewis,* Vol. 1, ed. Walter Hooper (New York: HarperCollins Publishers, Inc., 2004), 977.

3. *Time Magazine,* December 23, 1940, 38.

4. Victor E. Frankl, *Man's Search for Meaning* (New York: Washington Square Press, 1984), 98.

5. Jean Vanier, *Images of Love, Words of Hope* (Trosly, France: L'Arche Community).

6. Sören Kierkegaard, *Fear and Trembling and the Sickness Unto Death* (Princeton, NJ: Princeton University Press, 1974), 57.

7. J. R. R. Tolkien, "On Fairy-Stories," in *The Tolkien Reader* (New York: Ballantine Books, 1966), 85–86.

8. C. S. Lewis, *The Abolition of Man* (New York: Macmillan Publishers, 1943), 87–88.

9. Frankl, *Man's Search for Meaning,* 96.

10. Mother Teresa, *A Gift for God* (San Francisco: Harper and Row Publishers, 1975), 19.

11. Mother Teresa, *A Simple Path,* compiled by Lucinda Vardey (New York: Ballantine Books, 1995), 79.

12. G. K. Chesterton, *Orthodoxy* (San Francisco: Ignatius Press, reprint, 1908), 33.

13. Humphrey Carpenter, ed., *The Letters of J. R. R. Tolkien* (Boston: Houghton Mifflin Company, 1981), 201.

14. David Colbert, *The Magical World of The Lord of the Rings* (New York: Berkley Books, 2002), 108.

15. Fulton Sheen, *Simple Truths* (Liguori, MO: Liguori/Triumph, 1998), 55.

16. David Mills, "The Writer of Our Story," *Touchstone* Magazine, January/February 2002 (available at touchstonemag.com/archives/ The Writer of Our Story—under the subheading: "Gollum's Final Treachery").